Choosing a Career in
International Development

A Practical Guide to Working in the Professions of International Development

Donovan Russell

"Choosing a Career in International Development: A Practical Guide to Working in the Professions of International Development," by Donovan Russell. ISBN 978-1-62137-363-6 (Softcover) ISBN 978-1-62137-364-3 (Ebook).

Library of Congress Number: 2013915883.

Manufactured in the United States of America.

To my wife, Carol A. Russell

Contents

Foreword

This book discusses what it means to work in the various fields of International Development. It was written to help answer questions like: What exactly is International Development? What does one do when working in it? What skills and knowledge are required? What are the careers and positions in International Development and what are the responsibilities of those who hold them? What are the relationships of people who work in International Development to donor agencies and countries where projects are carried out? What are their relationships to international organizations, companies, NGO's, Universities, and other organizations that manage donor funded development projects? What are the rewards of working in International Development? What are the downsides to such work? How can one best prepare for it?

I have known the author for many years. His vast experience makes him highly qualified to write this book which provides practical down to earth information for students and people who are thinking about a change in career. It is also meant for those who teach or advise students and for international development specialists and administrators. While the book addresses specific sectors, it is written in such a way that it will be of use to those who have an interest in any of the fields of development. It addresses not only what International Development is but also the various ways that it is carried out. The views of both development specialists and host countries are discussed and explained. A message that comes through in various sections speaks to how a career in development can affect one's professional and personal lives.

The book is written in normal expository style interspersed with descriptions of real life conditions and traditions, real life development stories, and the actual challenges of various development initiatives. It speaks to conditions that are favorable to development and discusses their interconnectedness. It discusses categories of development and expresses views on how it should be approached. Of special interest are the perspectives of local hosts on development initiatives together with thoughts as to why these views are held. Using voices from host countries, the book speaks about cultures, explaining how they affect the work of development specialists and host country partners.

The author provides views on why individuals, organizations, and governments are involved in development. There is discussion on how different approaches to development grow out of differing interests and motivations. Several of these approaches are described. The author lists strategies, steps, and exercises that readers may follow in order to decide what, within International Development, they are most interested in and suited for. This includes reflection on who one is and what they believe related to kinds of work and to approaches in their field of interest.

The author also explains the steps that are taken while a project is formulated. This should help students who have chosen development as a career to better prepare. Also, for the benefit of those preparing, the author describes various types of organization that engage in development work.

The book describes specific sectors, or fields, and discusses them in terms of available careers and positions. Parts of the book indicate how initiatives in a sector may come together towards the solution of a major national problem. The book discusses how local conditions affect project work and notes the many kinds of action a development project may employ.

The chapter labeled "Working in Education" describes real life problems faced by a nation and challenges readers with exercise tasks whereby they conceptualize a development intervention, develop a strategy, determine steps that must be taken to operationalize a project, imagine working through approvals with stakeholders, organize staff and other resources that will be needed, coordinate with local institutions, design a project communications plan, develop an implementation plan, and manage supervision and monitoring. Each task is described in detail and readers are asked to relate these responsibilities to the experiential and academic background they would like to have. This section of the book also describes short to long term assignments one might be given, including everything from leading a major team to carrying out a one person research effort. True to life vignettes are used in the Education chapter (and in other chapters) to bring these challenges to life.

Each of the chapters that describe a sector are stylistically somewhat different. In their own way, the chapters provide information on a field, list examples of specific development positions, discuss coming face to face with one's assignment, speak to attitudes that can be helpful, note approaches to work, discuss how various organizations proceed with their work, call attention to strides made in the field, and point out why development continues to be vital to our future. Some of this is presented through real life situations and heart to heart story dialogue. There is discussion throughout the book on special challenges for development professionals and development teams. There are also listings of organizations which are engaged in International Development. The final chapter brings one back to the reason that Dr. Russell wrote the book and to the central question for readers. It is labeled "Character, Beliefs, Convictions and Practices, Is this Career for Me?"

Kanthie Athukorala, Ed.D. Assistant Professor, Sustainable Development Studies

School for International Training, Graduate Institute, Brattleboro, Vermont

Introduction

The intent of this book is to provide a practical down to earth description of international development that is useful to people who are considering whether or not to make it a career.

There are many ways of looking at international development. One approach views it in the context of human development, i.e. the development of a better quality of life for individuals. The many initiatives in the field, e.g. in healthcare, education, gender equality, human rights, disaster preparedness, environmental care, agricultural improvement, community development, conflict mitigation, democratization, institution building, infrastructure development, shelter, water and sanitation, vocational training, improved conditions for small business, economic reform, structural adjustment etc., are seen from the point of view of improving the human condition. This kind of thinking will be a foundation for much of what is presented in the book.

"Human development, as an approach, is concerned with what I take to be the basic development idea: namely, advancing the richness of human life, rather than the richness of the economy in which human beings live, which is only a part of it."[1]

"The basic purpose of development is to enlarge people's choices. People often value achievements that do not show up immediately, in income or growth figures, e.g. greater access to knowledge, better nutrition and health services, more secure livelihoods, security against crime and physical violence, satisfying leisure hours, political and cultural freedoms, and sense of participation in community activities. The objective of development is to create an enabling environment for people to enjoy long, healthy, and creative lives."[2]

Whatever your specialty, viewing development through the scope of human development is useful because that is what the enterprise is ultimately about. As development specialists take on new levels of responsibility over the course of a career, which remove them from the reward of interaction with local counterparts, communities, institutions, enterprises, and local colleagues, it is quite possible to lose sight of international development as basically human development.

If indeed you go into one of the fields of international development and have the opportunity of shoulder to shoulder work with your hosts under local conditions, you will be working on human development – be it research and planning together, teaching together, counseling together, performing health procedures together, advocating together, organizing together, building together, developing proposals together, evaluating together or budgeting and managing together. As well as the contributions you will make, life for you will be a great and fulfilling adventure. You will make close and valued friendships across rich cultural divides; friendships that will last always. And you will have the privilege of assisting people who desperately need help. But with all that you contribute through your work and through the friendships that you make, in the end you will find that you gained overwhelmingly more than you gave. Your life in development work will give you an opportunity to see and understand the needs – but also the great strengths of people who have a very different background from you. In addition, having challenging responsibilities in a different culture will result in your gaining significant new social, psychological, managerial, and technical strengths.

Because development work is cross cultural, it will give you an opportunity to see yourself more accurately and assess you own character in terms of fundamentals like egocentrism, paternalism, trust, empathy, decision making, problem solving, and feelings about the inherent worth of others. It will give you an opportunity to receive the experiential benefits of the world's diversity and become truly engaged in critical issues, some of them having life and death importance. It will provide you with input that is critical to gaining a better understanding of interdependencies across the world's natural, social, cultural, economic, and political environments. You will have opportunities to absorb that you would not otherwise have, learning on matters of knowledge and sharing, on matters of respect, appreciation, communications, humility, and the place of mankind in programs and projects – either at the center of consideration – or secondary to the impersonal models, systems, plans, and bureaucracies that sometimes permeate our work. You will have opportunities to become one with other places and peoples, where you and they come to truly want the best for the other. And unlike other work, you will have the opportunity, if you so choose, to experience the vulnerability of those you serve; to be alive to shared humanity. Development work gives you a chance to truly get next to the world's challenges. It leads to striking insights on the sometimes jarring realities you come to know. It also promotes an identification with and love for other peoples and places. Read for example, the paragraph that follows by a development professional who is leaving a place and a people he has come to know, love, and respect:

"Look, look from this rooftop of Africa, look from this Cathedral like pinnacle in the Mountain Kingdom. Look down silent canyons, toward Transkei, toward Natal, toward the Eastern Cape. Listen, listen to the wind, listen to revered ancestors watching over their people and whispering of new arrivals. Listen in the wind for a place where people have time for each other and there is security in family and community. Where there is respect and courtesy between the generations and fundamental sharing is still a virtue. Where life is a spiritual thing and being is as important as doing or having. What does the wind say about a place such as this? What does it foretell?"[3]

1. *Amaryta Sen, Human Development Report, New York, United Nations, 1990, p.1*
2. *Mahbub ul Haq, Human Development Report, New York, United Nations, 1990, p.1*
3. *Donovan Russell, Right Before His Very Eyes, New York, Writers Showcase, 2001, p.ix*

Personal Statement

There are a great many reasons that individuals, organizations, nations, and international agencies work in international development. To illustrate the need and urgency, I will speak to some of the more dramatic and compelling reasons in the following section.

"For I was hungry and you gave me something to eat, I was thirsty and you gave me drink; I was a stranger and you invited me in."[1]

Human Development

The UN Human Development Report[2] provides startling information on global undernourishment, e.g. Eritrea 73%, Republic of the Congo 71%, Burundi 68%, Tajikistan 61%, Sierra Leone 50%, and Zambia 49%. Hunger and poverty are not stand alone conditions. They exist where there is lack of opportunity and where there is social inequality. In turn, the debility of hunger and poverty keeps people from overcoming disadvantage and from accessing opportunity. Charitable relief is important but is a temporary palliative. If root causes are not addressed, hunger returns. Someone has said that when we attend to the needs of those in want, we give them what belongs to them. More than performing works of mercy, we are paying a debt of justice.

The following points out major causes of abject poverty. Allow me to share an actual account. My local office mate was quiet that morning. When I asked what was wrong, he told me that a young boy who worked on his grandfather's farm had committed suicide the night before because he failed his grade seven leaving exam. That's how important education is as a possible escape from the disadvantages some families have experienced for generations. I have been in countries across Africa, Asia, and the Middle East over the past 35 years, working on projects to help people gain at least some education. One of those projects aims to enhance opportunities by constructing more schools and by improving teaching practices, instructional materials, supervision, parental participation, and funding. It works to ensure access for all and to upgrade the quality of instruction. The task is huge. This is a country of 135 million people packed into an area the size of Wisconsin. In the five primary grades, there are nearly 18 million students, 78,000 schools, and 300,000 teachers. Official enrollment has increased rapidly over the last ten years but conditions in the schools make parents wonder if their children would be better off at home. Only about half get to grade five. One of the more disadvantaged schools might be characterized by 80 to 100 children per teacher, no working toilets, running water, electricity, windows, heating or cooling, practically no instructional supplies, and unqualified teachers whose practices discourage students. Discrimination against certain ethnic groups and girls is common in some parts of the country. Children may have school for only two to three hours and classes often start late and close early because children have to walk great distances. Many teachers and students are absent – a function of the necessity for children to work at home and for teachers to have other jobs or small businesses.

One can describe equally unfortunate conditions in other parts of the lives of the poor in their housing, water and sanitation, air quality, food, etc. In the capital city, I regularly walked past a park. Women lived in the tall grass there with their children. They bathed, washed clothes, and drank from a polluted lake. A main source of their food was handouts. The air was deadly. Children from the park would follow me on crowded streets and across heavy traffic, crying for more than I had to give. Their weakened conditions left them susceptible to disease. One crippled young man would spot me and follow through the crowded blocks on hands and knees. These people spend every waking hour searching for food. They are trapped on the survival level of Maslow's hierarchy of human motivation. It's unfair that the extremely poor never have a chance at anything even approaching self-actualization and dignity. They are powerless and routinely suffer social and economic discrimination.

I vividly remember too, street women in another country who were so desperate they inflicted burns on their naked children, hoping to attract the sympathy of strangers who could help with food. Near starvation had stunted their children. No doubt they would not be just physically stunted. Psychological and cognitive stunting would happen and energy would be sapped. They would be easy prey for disease and many would eventually die from ordinary diarrhea. In much of Asia, one can witness an environment stressed to the breaking point by population, something which once led to the disappearance of civilizations in other parts of the world. For example, in Nepal, erosion has washed away the soil of many subsistence farmers, people who had only an acre or so to begin with. In Bangladesh, millions have no choice but to drink arsenic laden water because that is what is in their wells. Millions of children in much of the developing world should be wearing masks against eventual respiratory sickness. And in Africa, I recall the poor rural women of

Lesotho, Ethiopia, and Mali who carry water every day for hours, leaving little time or energy for anything else. Being so close to the edge of existence in these countries leaves them defenseless in times of drought, flood, malaria, or dengue fever.

The situation for the privileged in underdeveloped countries is dramatically different. There are millionaires in the poorest of them, while others live outside the formal economy, having virtually no cash at all. The privileged are not in the public schools. Like their parents before them, they are in good private schools at home or abroad. They will become the country's professional and business leaders. Poor education is just one factor associated with poverty and hunger. There are many others. Each is both cause and effect. For example, poverty is a major reason that schools are disadvantaged and lacking education is one reason that societies are poor. Poverty is responsible in large part for inadequate health care and poor health contributes to poverty. *Peace is necessary to a society being able to work toward development and development is an important condition for stability and peace.* "If you want peace, work for justice,"[3] wrote Paul the VI.

The UN Human Development Report and other resources provide data containing clues to a peoples' condition. A study of the factors involved is a start in unraveling causes and identifying remedies. Solutions have to address systemic, structural, and even cultural matters. Being at the bottom for generations seems to make people think that is where they are supposed to be. Many interrelated factors contribute to hunger and poverty, e.g. culture, beliefs, traditions, the role and treatment of women, priorities in public spending, labor rights and practices, land tenure and use, natural resources and the environment, technology diffusion, the structure of trade and trade policies, corruption and crime, security, labor productivity, political stability, bureaucratic efficiency, demographics, human rights, leadership, and governance. It is not because we are smarter or more virtuous that we live in privilege. The extremely poor I have known are intelligent, gracious, and good. In this interdependent world we are sometimes privileged because they are exploited. And we, not they, have the ability to change things.

---

1. *Matthew 25:35*
2. *UN Human Development Report, New York, United Nations, 2006*
3. *John P. Hogan, Credible Signs of Christ Alive, New York, Rowman and Littlefield, 2003, p. ix*

Chapter I
International Development

Separate and Complementary

*T*he two most common divisions in development are not set apart in the book's chapters. For the record though, they are (1) disaster relief and humanitarian aid and (2) international development. Disaster relief and humanitarian assistance are usually short term efforts related to immediate crisis events. They may well have elements of longer term and more sustainable development, especially as they are re-designed during an evolving crisis. International development, on the other hand, is usually thought of as dealing with longer term and deeply imbedded issues. It deals with issues of several related types. It is not crisis focused, although by comparison to areas of the world with less vexing problems, the problems it addresses are indeed sometimes crises. When reference is made to international development in this book, it may be to either disaster relief and humanitarian aid or to longer term and multi-faceted development. Often, a specific challenge in development will have elements of both immediate disaster and long term problems. A comprehensive development project may be designed to address all of the challenges of the situation whether they are closely interrelated or not and will therefore, have initiatives of both short term and long term duration.

Common Considerations

Sustainability is a key concept in this field and a truly sustainable development project is one which will be able to carry on, once international involvement has ceased. Sustainability can relate to efforts under both disaster relief and longer term international development projects, although it usually has a higher profile in the design of a regular development project. A sustainable project takes account of economic, environmental, and social factors in organizing initiatives which are not dependent on temporary resources. A sustainable initiative will not be dependent on more natural resources than the environment can provide, more financial resources than will be available from usual sources, more technical abilities than will be available when the project is finished, or more civic support than the community and stakeholders will generate on a continuous basis.

International development efforts may consist of a single project to address a fairly well-defined societal problem or a series of distinct projects that are targeted on separate but related problems in society. In the latter, the effort may be sequenced or folded into a single large and multifaceted program of coordinated projects.

Integrated development may employ involved problem solving initiatives that address a problem from various points of view, e.g. human behaviors and attitudes, habits, culture, politics, economic practices, management attitudes and practices, etc. Integrated development may be rolling and perhaps never ending as it becomes obvious that the solving of one problem in a society or institution is dependent on solving another. In a truly aspiring community, this may go on and on. Success may give rise to further initiatives that are inspired by accomplishment. It could be for example, that to address what at first is thought to be a straight economic policy problem, a project might discover that it needs to become involved in the empowerment of local women, environmental management, issues of accountability, matters of class favoritism, or all of these.

Top down and bottom up – There is of course the concept that development is most successfully addressed from the top through adoption and internalization by host institutions of policy initiatives. Parallel to this is the long standing conviction that development is most successful when it is bottom up through, for example, interactive dialogue and instruction, organizational development, education for critical consciousness, cooperative work, community endeavors, etc. While development specialists may disagree on the relative importance of each, most projects employ both top down and bottom up initiatives during practical implementation, even if not in original design.

Equality has become one of the main goals of most development programs and projects. It has become accepted that inequality within an institution, organization, community, or nation can generate poverty and related conditions. Inequality of access for instance, can have a serious impact on level of education attained, skill acquisition, personal health, shelter, type of employment, income level, rights, and social or political participation in a community or nation.

Participation is a primary factor in international development because it is the key to a clear view of needs and realistic aspirations. It is also the key to reasonable project design, host ownership of project goals and activities, appropriate and meaningful execution of project actions, institutional, community, and government support, and local empowerment and sustainability.

Rights based development's main goal is the strengthening of those less than fully empowered and promotes the opening to fair opportunity for all groups. It stands for the development of individual, community, institutional, organizational, and governmental capacities in the interest of maximum achievement and full benefit. It works for removal of inhibitors to rights and opportunities and promotes movement toward full personal potential.

Capacity building accompanies most development project goals. It furthers the ability of individuals, leaders, institutions, organizations, businesses, and governments to manage effectively and efficiently. It attempts to enable. It may deal with the upgrading of legal or contract frameworks, address dozens of policies and functions within an institution, or, in contrast, with the behaviors of employees related to responsibilities and position descriptions. It may address strategies, budgeting, scheduling, motivation and rewards, evaluation, management styles, and any number of things in order that capacity to accomplish as desired is fulfilled.

Sectors are the common areas of development work and usually correspond with the major areas of endeavor by governments. Development projects often work within a subsector, e.g. Nursing Education within the Health Sector, Vocational Education within the Education Sector, or Aviation within the Transportation Sector. Sometimes a project will work in every subsector of a government sector. In some cases, a project may work in more than one sector at the same time, e.g. Transportation and Immigration. Some of the major sectors of work in international development are Education, Health, Environment, Agriculture, Urban Planning and Administration, Finance, Justice and Human Rights, Labor, Water and Sanitation, Shelter, Disaster Relief, and Refugee Assistance.

Strategy, Planning, and Assessment – Many good management tools are commonly used in international development, e.g. basic research, country assessments, goal development, sector assessments, country strategies, project identification, project assistance plans, thorough requests for proposals, detailed proposals on what is to be done, and how, and to what degree, logical frameworks to integrate, coordinate and guide actions, and work plans. There are also guides on suggested international standards. Many national development agencies have them as do other bodies such as Regional Development Banks, UN Agencies, the World Bank, the International Monetary Fund, etc.

A widespread initiative – On September 18, 2000, the UN General Assembly adopted resolution 55/2: United Nations Millennium Declaration.[1] The declaration was broad and encompassing. Among the issues it addressed were world development goals. One-hundred eighty-nine nations made a promise to free people from extreme poverty and multiple deprivations. The pledge turned into eight Millennium Development Goals, some to be accomplished by 2015 and some to be completed by 2020. They are:

(1) Eradicate extreme poverty and hunger
(2) Achieve universal primary education
(3) Promote gender equality and empower women
(4) Reduce child mortality
(5) Improve maternal health
(6) Combat HIV/AIDS, malaria, and other diseases
(7) Ensure environmental sustainability
(8) Develop a global partnership for development.

---

1. The Millennium Development Goals, New York, UNDP, 2000

Chapter II
A Complex and Worthy Profession

F actors that go beyond those usually considered when development projects are implemented can make a project worthwhile or if ignored, significantly reduce its potential. Much in overseas development is managed in western business-like ways. This is understandable and natural given the orientation of most donors. But it can blind us to subtle considerations that if overlooked, make our efforts less worthwhile than they would otherwise be.

A Host Country View

Let us imagine what a Deputy Minister of Education whose nation is a place of majestic river valleys, silent canyons, and stately mountains might have said when addressing host country and expatriate professionals early in a nationwide development project. His message might have been this:

"Improvement in education has to happen through my country's social and political milieu and administrative culture. To be sustained, it has to be imbedded in our consciousness and in our institutions. It cannot be treated in isolation from our way of looking at things or the everyday concerns and interests of our communities. In our work together, we will have to look beyond the usual researched reasons for such things as inequity,

6

ineffectiveness, inadequacy, inefficiency, irrelevance, and poor quality."[1] He might have gone on to say, "Development in this country cannot be done through technical interventions only. Project successes will not be sustained unless they have been cooperatively planted and nurtured long enough to have deep roots. Long and gentle nurturing will have to be done by credible helpers, both local and others, who know our people and their ways, and who know how to make things happen here. A donor's need to pursue predetermined deliverables can cause implementers to take actions yielding only temporary success. Lasting impact will necessitate attention to deep non-technical matters. The cultural, social, political, and personal must be factored into our work together. A technically excellent intervention can fail without this. A technically less desirable intervention can succeed, given the right human approach."[2]

What did the Deputy Minister mean? One could write a book on this but let us briefly reflect on it. Important and impressive things continue to be accomplished in overseas development. Of course there is always room for improvement. Doing things in ways that make them sustainable is high on our list of goals. It is by far best if interventions can be put into place in a way that gives people a chance to take them as their own. This is a complicated challenge and it is this to which the Deputy Minister was referring.

Implications

Development demands a lot from those involved. If we do not understand the country in which we are working and have not established trusting relationships, we will likely proceed in unproductive ignorance. Each development setting is unique. However, in the traditional setting being spoken of here, people are born into place and position, rules are inherited, things are done in very personal ways, change can be threatening to the web of life, looking out for one's own is a duty, work, and even business sometimes takes second place to social process, decisions for the modern sector may be mysteriously made by someone outside of its formal structure, sharing goes beyond our concept of it, individualism may not be seen as we see it, communities strive for consensus – sometimes even at the expense of progress, materialism is not a significant value, productivity is governed in mysterious ways, and a distinctive sensory environment and history are revered and exert much influence.

It is important in this setting then, that development initiatives be given time to achieve legitimacy and credibility, that counterparts achieve relationships which can facilitate action, that verbal protocols and written agreements be understood, and that interventions are introduced in such a way that they can become accepted and ultimately valued.

It is important as well, that development partners know how to proceed in ways that strengthen rather than strain host institutions. In part, this demands that development specialists understand the cultural range of their counterpart's possible actions and decision making and know how to get things done through the country's traditional as well as modern factions.

It is important too, that development initiatives start at an appropriate size and scale up as understanding and institutions mature. Needless to say this requires considerable awareness of the situation. Just being sophisticated enough to recognize whether an agreement has been truly reached can be challenging. All of this needs to be done without abdicating the professional role and responsibility for which a development specialist has been employed.

Getting a true meeting of minds in a culturally alien setting can be misunderstood. With the possibility that the cultural divide between developed and developing societies may be growing, sensitivity based on true interest, close engagement, and caring can be the difference between success or failure. An expedient one sided approach may seemingly get things done but is not likely to facilitate sustainable progress.

In this setting too, it is critical to somehow match the stream of tradition and wisdom which supports a way of life with the river of inputs and initiatives that a modern development project can bring. It is too easy to overlook the reluctant voice of one's hosts and to be oblivious to local perspectives and motivations.

Also, it is important to understand the complexity of internalizing a cause or innovation. One needs to somehow learn what may be too alien or too far removed from what is allowed of his or her hosts.

Development managers do well to recognize that individuals and groups in every setting are at various places on a social continuum and are at different places in confidence. A development specialist's ability to perceive and understand this is dependent on sincere interaction with colleagues, interaction that achieves trust based on respect and that allows communication and exploration beyond cultural boundaries.

These are considerations for professionals who would make the development process come alive for local colleagues, institutions, and communities. It would be based on what is truly meaningful to those colleagues. Bringing about this sort of thing is fascinating and enormously rewarding. The Deputy Minister was making a case for this kind of thoughtful approach. Let us reflect a bit further on a thoughtful approach in the points below.

For a project to succeed and be sustained, host country people must become willing, able, and organized to eventually manage reforms themselves. Some development organizations overlook this. This removes the opportunity for a people to display initiative and to feel responsible. It can contribute to an unseen and long term psychological dependency and can inhibit development from actually happening. It is important that professionals in development understand this.

For the most part, development professionals believe in genuine host participation. However, some professionals can be overwhelmed by the momentum of the organization which employs them. Excessive momentum can be generated by themes of development that are in vogue in the profession, by the influence of outside policy research, new techniques and technologies, and new theories of management. There is also the situation where expected outcomes are unrealistic, making it difficult for a development specialist or manager to employ participatory methods. Regular forthright communications between a development specialist or manager and the home office can go a long way toward remedying this.

Host country people cannot work meaningfully toward a development unless they have time to cope with its complexity, understand the organization it will require, and perceive an outcome that is compatible with their values. This is a very important consideration at the time of project design. It also argues for field specialists who have the ability to painstakingly revise projects in concert with home offices, donors, and host country participants.

Changing agendas imposed from outside can promote vertical allegiances that divert local attention from the horizontal person to person, institution to institution, and community to community collaboration that is critical to local decision making, ownership, self-reliance, and sustainability. Regular and forthright communications between a development specialist or manager and the home office can go a long way toward obviating excessive interference of this kind.

Laid on bought and paid for development as opposed to deep rooted, shoulder to shoulder development, can mislead donors about accomplishment, leading them to short cut the time that true development takes.

A cafeteria style of development can lead to a periodic taking up of new themes before participants are ready, unrealistically raising expectations only to demoralize participants when an effort is replaced with something else. This is contrary to the systematic laying of foundations and the accomplishment of conditions necessary to being able to take the next steps in appropriate measure and at the appropriate time. However, if used in an enlightened way, this kind of intervention does not have to be destructive.

People can only work productively in accordance with their readiness and preparation. As in anything, it is necessary to become fully accomplished at a level before being able to go further. Also, if an initiative employs techniques or resources that are not going to be available when a donor has finished, hosts will not be able to make it theirs and sustain it. Working outside the long term capability of one's hosts can create unreal expectations and set them up for failure.

Bringing about meaningful, appropriate, and sustained change requires credibility. Creditability in development is generated by true partnerships where the problems and dilemmas of a people are understood and taken on through close and longstanding association, as if they were problems and dilemmas of the assistance personnel.

It is critical in development that host country people gain belief in themselves and faith in the predictability and the possibility of accomplishment. That cannot be achieved from an expert's reports or preassembled donor funds.

1. Comments on a Basic and Non-Formal Education Systems Project, Donovan Russell in a talk at Cornell Institute for Public Affairs, Cornell University, Ithaca, New York, 2010.
2. Ibid

Chapter III
Reasons that Individuals, Organizations, and Governments are Involved in International Development

Why There Is Interest

W hy is there an interest in bringing about change through developed activities? There are many motives. It is probable that advocates of development hold more than one of these. Perhaps most who have an interest simply feel that it is not right that people anywhere have to live without adequate food or that they lack basic nutrition, water, medicine, healthcare, shelter, clothing, education, jobs, or sanitation. Some may have different interests, being concerned for example, that so many people are denied free speech, the right to assemble, police protection from crime, and an impartial court system. Still, others may believe it is just not right that millions receive practically nothing for their labor, or that so many have no access to credit or banking. And at a more basic level, others may be concerned that there are millions of refugees or people in disastrous prisons with no hope of being released. There are a great many reasons that individuals in the so called developed world are concerned about the situation of people in less fortunate places. Incidentally, it is not correct to assume that development concerns and initiatives are only from developed to less developed countries. Increasingly, the concern, initiative, and leadership for development reside within the very countries that need change.

Why Organizations Participate in Development

International development efforts, for the most part, are the domain of organizations rather than individuals. There are hundreds of non-governmental organizations around the world, each with its view of what should be given priority in international development. There are many religious organizations (Christian, Muslim, Jewish, Buddhist, Hindu, and others) that give attention to development needs. There are professional groups which have accepted a development challenge, e.g. organizations representing doctors and other healthcare professionals, teachers and other educators, lawyers, judges and court system administrators, business managers and owners, labor advocates, agriculturalists, environmental conservationists, and community development professionals. Governments get deeply involved as well, each with its own reason for doing so. International organizations like The World Bank, The Asian Development Bank, other regional development banks, The International Monetary Fund, The World Trade Organization, The World Health Organization, and the UN Agencies do a large amount of work in the field on behalf of the world's governments.

There are organizations that believe fairness, due process, equal rights, and equal opportunity should be extended to the entire human family. There are others that maintain everyone should have a reasonable standard of living. Some of these would have the poor lifted up so that they become good consumers. Others see it differently, believing that to make the poor just good consumers is to sell them short and that development should be more than that. There are organizations which believe the poor and disenfranchised are being misused as cheap instruments of production and that they need, in some way, to be liberated, even if that just starts with liberating their thinking.

In the world of commerce, business interests are keenly interested in an ordered business-like environment. Some commercial interests may think it is only right and fair that people everywhere have equal opportunities to excel and to live decently. Others are likely to believe that opportunities which help the world's poor become more skilled, better educated, healthier, better off economically, and more sophisticated, contribute to consumer reliability and business predictability.

There are organizations which strongly believe that the world will be troubled and at war, as long as some are healthy while many are not, some are free while others are nearly slaves, some are rich while many are poverty stricken, and some can read and write while many cannot.

There are also organizations, e.g. the U.S. Peace Corps, which believe that to know the situation of other peoples, to understand and to be involved with them, even from a distance, is to make one's own nation stronger and more enduring. This too is a motive for involvement.

It is only normal as well, that political interests would enter into the mix of motives. Given the reality of nation state power, related to who benefits from the world's resources, there are other motives for being concerned about international development. Nations which are engaged in development efforts have mixed motives. Some of these are probably quite altruistic while some are related to promoting and safeguarding their own interests. Perhaps in most cases there is a mix of these two basic motives.

At a different level, there are no doubt idealists who have a conviction that everyone's inheritance should be recognized. It is said that because mankind's consciousness has evolved over the centuries, from a sort of reactive intelligence to self-sufficiency through individuation and then to more and more enlightened oneness, it is just natural for people in fortunate circumstances to care about the less fortunate. Some, who care about human potential, believe it is everyone's right as a human being to get out from under having to labor most of every day just to sustain their families and keep them secure. They believe that it should be in everyone's inheritance to be able to create, to have self-pride, and to actualize their potential.

One could go on about the motives of individuals and organizations that are active in international development. Certainly the list above is not exhaustive.

And so there is a great host of organizations working in international development, some targeting their initiatives toward children, others toward women, the illiterate, untouchables and other socially disadvantaged people, toward orphans, the physically impaired, the rural poor, the urban poor, and many others, including entire sectors of whole nations. Each of these organizations has its' own set of reasons for doing so.

Different Approaches Grow From Differing Views

Speculation about motive is important to understanding why there are significant development efforts across the world and why organizations emphasize the things they do. It is of interest to note that each actor in the field has its own view on the best way to go about development. That view stems from experiences and from the values held by participating organizations. Development organizations attempt to bring about change in several ways, for example:

(1) Through national and sub-national institutions.
(2) Through the encouragement of individual behavioral change.
(3) By addressing development challenges as a matter of sharing specific techniques.
(4) By encouraging social and/or political change.
(5) By undertaking relief and rescue missions.
(6) By helping their hosts develop their own capacity to cope with challenges.
(7) By understand and treating development as a continuing process.
(8) By bringing about specifically defined achievements through carefully designed projects.
(9) By advocating on behalf of a target group, e.g. children.
(10) By influencing government policies, e.g. on health care, basic education, trade rules.
(11) By concentrating on participatory and action research.
(12) By contributing well trained volunteers who help hosts address pressing needs.
(13) By providing highly specialized technical consultants to address difficult issues.
(14) Through the provision of infrastructure e.g. roads, airports or dams.
(15) By organizing well focused and specialized training in certain sectors.

A BASIC SHIFT IN APPROACH

In recent years, there has been a change by some of the organizations which undertake large multifaceted national development, from what has been called *project assistance to program assistance.*

In traditional project development, there are teams of select personnel who operate somewhat independently, i.e. in cooperation with a host system but also with resources and capabilities of their own. Projects usually operate in accordance with defined inputs and timed objectives. They are routinely monitored and evaluated against agreed upon standards of achievement and are accountable to their sources of funding. It is not uncommon for several projects to operate side by side in a sector. Because these are often funded by different donors, have distinct objectives, and have management teams of their own, they often fail to coordinate and can inadvertently have the effect of dividing the attention of host institutions or organizations. They have strong advantages as well.

Program Assistance is an effort to overcome lack of coordination and cooperation and to strengthen the capacity of host governments and their institutions. Donors agree to combine their efforts under the leadership of the host managers. The intent is to put host country personnel in charge, with the assistance of technical advisors, and to engage them in such a way that efforts and resources are used to address needs and agendas as defined in a true partnership. The idea is to operate in such a way that confidence is built, ownership is felt, skills and management capacities are developed, and achievements are sustained. It is a complicated approach with substantial challenges, demanding considerable patience. Some feel that a combination of traditional project assistance together with some form of program assistance should be used.

Professional organizations which routinely carry out development work on behalf of donors and host countries have experienced individuals working for them. Some of these organizations are not for profit, some are consulting firms and some are Universities. Perhaps it would be helpful if there were ways for these experienced professionals to be more influential with respect to project design.

ANOTHER APPROACH

It would be a significant oversight to omit one other distinctive approach. It is referred to as *Integrated Community Development.* There are organizations that see development as a continuous process whereby reliable long-term support is provided to communities and organizations in accordance with evolving needs. The process is not limited to a specific sector but engages in whatever is needed as a community progresses. If an undertaking by a community necessitates specialized training, it is arranged. If later on it is necessary to set up a cooperative to produce something, then that is facilitated. If a source of credit becomes necessary, it is undertaken. Development initiatives are problem solving by nature. Being a process approach, the importance of taking time for community readiness and preparation is recognized. Full participation and internalization are important. The trust and credibility that grows from meaningful partnership in ventures decided upon by participants, is valued. All assistance is functional, i.e. executed so that a community or organization itself can accomplish something they have decided on – whether that is a village water system, community gardens, a farm to market road, better schooling for their children, or a village health center. The process undertakes problem solving to address aspirations and builds on success to induce further aspirations. A major strength of this approach is that because accomplishment is by host participants, it should be sustainable. However, this approach is hard to accept for donor organizations that operate in accordance with a culture which embraces agreed on inputs and processes toward achievement of defined and measurable goals, within set time frames. In actual fact, most organizations involved in international development probably believe in and utilize a variety of the approaches described above.

Chapter IV
Thoughts on Choosing a Career in International Development

International development is a multi-faceted field. A great many talented young (and not so young) people at least flirt with the possibility of engaging in it professionally. With the exception of a few students that have studied with economists, educators, health care professionals, and the like, and who have also worked for development agencies, most people probably have little understanding of what it is all about. How then might someone go about exploring development opportunities, and if they like what they see, how might they get into it? Allow me to outline some considerations that might be helpful.

General Description of the Field – The field contains an array of international agencies, government departments, contractor entities, volunteer groups, non-governmental organizations, education institutions, and others that are engaged for a variety of purposes and which approach international development at various levels using many different methods.

Two Extremes

(a) Depending on why a funding organization is engaged and what it wishes to accomplish, it might approach development by working with overseas governments and institutions through sophisticated multi-faceted projects awarded to contracted managers.

(b) At the extreme opposite, another organization might believe in a type of development that is accomplished by working with and through individuals. Both agendas might be broadly political, social, or economic.

Examples of Reasons for Engagement

(a) Some organizations in the field are enamored of and committed to sector wide development through technique and systems.

(b) Others may be committed to educating for human rights, justice, or something else.

(c) Some of the better known efforts in development are in basic relief and rescue.

(d) There are organizations whose sole function in development is advocacy, e.g. for better working conditions, the preservation of heritage, or democratic institutions. Other organizations are engaged in attempts to influence governments, perhaps through methods other than straight advocacy, on for example, healthcare practice, trade, the empowerment of regional and local authorities, or the care of refugees.

(e) Some development is basically infrastructure building roads, water systems, airports, schools, hospitals, etc., with capacity building for subsequent operations and ongoing costs. The above are illustrative. They are not necessarily stand-alone efforts, i.e. an organization or a consortium of organizations may at times engage in combinations of them.

Mechanisms of Engagement

Organizations engaged in development use a variety of delivery mechanisms. Some work through trained volunteers on carefully designed and targeted initiatives, some work through specialized long term technical assistance, some use short term consultants in key roles, while others recruit and work through local personnel. Because a particular initiative may need to address a variety of diverse objectives, it may use a combination of these. The design of an effort, including the type of assistance it utilizes, often has a relationship to an organization's beliefs and motives. Funding may also be a determinant.

(a) *Project Assistance* – Perhaps most traditional development has been through carefully designed and vetted development projects. These have time bound goals and objectives with defined measurable results, accomplished over a contracted period, using predetermined inputs in terms of activities, personnel, operating funds, and the like. A development project might be short term or multi-year. Although usually confined to a sector or part of a sector, a development project might address a wide array of objectives and have a budget of many millions of dollars. Those managing such efforts across cultures are well trained and experienced individuals. Complicated projects are contracted out by competitive bid to sophisticated organizations.

(b) *Buy in Assistance* – Donor nations and agencies sometimes promote other vehicles which are less than full project assistance, e.g. the establishment through competitive bid of specialized technical services which may be purchased cafeteria style.

(c) *Program Assistance* – While project assistance remains popular, a major innovation is the advent of program assistance. Here, a group of donor nations and agencies, together with a host country, combine efforts to address system wide challenges in a sector in a harmonized way. There is cooperative needs identification, design, and implementation. The idea is to reduce fragmented and poorly coordinated project efforts, to get more impact from pooled resources, to integrate management and abandon parallel initiatives, to use common standards, and through host country management, to increase potential for continuity and sustainability. These may embrace an entire sector of development in a country. One that I know well is a 1.2 billion dollar effort in South Asia. There are, of course, disadvantages as well as advantages to each model.

(d) *Integrated Development* – A quite different model of development is that of integrated community development. Unlike major nationwide projects and programs, these are much smaller community wide problem solving initiatives. Usually NGO financed and operated, these see development as a continuous and evolving process. They are needs-based in the sense that a community executes, with assistance, something needed in and of itself but also of importance to accomplishment longer term, of a more livable community with improved opportunities. By addressing barriers to community development, they can become quite diverse in focus and method. Because they are accomplished by host participants, the results should be quite sustainable.

A First Step in Deciding on a Career

Clarifying One's Interests – With this broad overview of the field as a backdrop, how might someone who finds it intriguing go about deciding what they would like to pursue? **First**, one might simply identify their passion in terms of specialty. For instance, the environment, energy, agriculture, natural resources, education planning, program development, teacher training, the law, economics, healthcare, urban development, microfinance, family planning, rural development, human rights, better government, housing, migration, refugee settlement, and so on. **Second**, one might consider target groups of interest, e.g. women and children, rural people, the grossly disadvantaged or disenfranchised, refugees, teachers, health workers, government officers, etc. **Third**, if possible, determine at least provisionally whether they are interested in field implementation or whether they prefer policy, design, or contract work at a headquarters in a developed city. Incidentally, my bias is that experience in the field is necessary to effectiveness later on if one decides on a career at headquarters. **Fourth**, even if at this point one is not very clear about it, begin research on the organizations that seem to match your interests in terms of what they do. This is not very difficult. For example, the website www.interaction.org, displays definitive information on a coalition of 180 non-governmental organizations.

A Second Step in Deciding on a Career

Matching Self With Characteristics of Place – If one is still unclear about working in the field, they might research cultures and places and then reflect on how they would likely react to major differences in human attitudes and practices pertaining to matters like time, space, formality, work, sharing, having, being, beginnings and endings, belonging, courtesy, modesty, tact, cordiality and to obvious human vulnerability, hunger, sickness, poverty, and lack of convenience. Hopefully if one is sincerely interested in development work, they will be willing to give it a try regardless of what they discover about matters like this. While coming face to face with and working through another culture can be confusing and frustrating, it is rewardingly broadening and character developing.

A Third Step in Deciding on a Career

Matching One's Values with Organizational Types – Assuming after these considerations that one wishes a field career, the next step would be to determine how you wish to operate. Here your values will come into play. What would fit your personality? What would be congruent with your beliefs about other people? What would match your view of what development should be? What are your true motives and what are the real motives of various organizations with whom you could work? At this point, your answers will be hazy. But it is an important exercise. There are hundreds of organizations working in international development. They vary greatly in terms of what they hold important, their beliefs about people, the themes, interests, and agendas they promote, and therefore approaches in their work.

CONCLUSION

Many types of entity work in international development, e.g. departments and agencies of national governments, offices of the UN and other international organizations, entities from many countries which work through volunteers like the Peace Corps, religious denominations, relief agencies, charities, regional development banks, labor unions, NGO's, university offices, foundations, contract specialist organizations, for profit companies, professional societies, and others. Each has its mission, its expertise, its level of operation, and its approaches. There are many possibilities for a person to explore who is considering a career in international development.

Norman Cousins was editor of the Saturday Review for more than thirty years and served as adjunct professor of psychiatry and bio-behavioral science at UCLA. Mr. Cousins was the recipient of the UN Peace Metal, the American Peace Award, and the Albert Schweitzer Award for Humanitarianism. To take this discussion on international development beyond the usual considerations in career planning, I will quote from his book, *The Celebration of Life*. "Each individual is capable of:

– Both great altruism and great venality. He has it within his means to extend the former and exorcise the latter.

– Both great compassion and great indifference. He has it within his means to nourish the former and outgrow the latter.

– Ennobling life and disfiguring it. He has it within his means to assert the former and anathematize the latter.

If he recognizes that his basic purpose is to justify his humanity, he will have no difficulty in addressing himself to these choices. Basic purpose and human destiny do not lie outside, but within him."[1]

A Simple Exercise for Preliminary Career Planning

Reflect on why you wish to work in international development.

Do a one paragraph statement on your internship or career objective.

List the three fields in which you have most expertise, e.g. Health, Education, Agriculture, Infrastructure Development, Economic Development, Finance, Business, Human Rights and Social Justice, Democratization, Conflict Resolution, Natural Resources, Climate, Food Security, Disaster Relief, Refugee Settlement, Project Preparation and Evaluation, Women in Development, Gender Issues, Community Organization, etc.

Describe the specific expertise you have related to each of the three general fields, e.g. in Education it might be adult literacy, for Health it might be HIV Aids, for Infrastructure Development it might be Architecture.

Identify organizations that specialize in the specific fields you have listed.

Reflect on academic preparation in relationship to your career objectives.

List the general part of the world you have most interest in working. List the countries within this that most interest you. Ask yourself why.

Research development work that is ongoing in the countries that you have listed.

Consider your understanding of how development work is organized, e.g. do you have a general understanding at this point of program assistance, of general project assistance with one focus under one agency, general project assistance with a complex focus done cooperatively by more than one agency or contractor, of specialty buy in work, of refugee or disaster relief work, of general community development, how NGO's work, and of how volunteer organizations work?

Consider the type of organization that you believe would most interest you at this point, e.g. a major international donor, a bilateral agency, a contract organization, an NGO, a relief organization, a religious charitable organization, a volunteer agency, etc.

---

1. Norman Cousin, The Celebration of Life, New York, Harper and Row, 1974, p. 72.

Chapter V
Development Opportunities Do Not Just Happen

There are, of course, many types of development work. Some development organizations have a more or less unilateral focus. If you are inclined toward the mission they embrace and the way in which they approach their work, you will wish to keep up with their initiatives and look for an opportunity to become involved with them. For example, one organization identifies promising local people who have dreams and aspirations that require assistance. Its goal is to help aspiring people become effective entrepreneurs able to turn aspirations into profitable businesses. The idea is that ignited business in a demoralized and backward community can spark community wide development. Imagining the kind of knowledge and skills that would allow you to participate may not be hard if you have a business background. But to be sure, you will want to talk with these kinds of development organizations as soon as possible, i.e. while you are still preparing yourself with education and practical experience.

The range of specialized work is broad. For example, some organizations recruit teachers for overseas schools or businesses where there is a need to provide English language instruction or perhaps business management instruction, or especially good math and science teaching. Some may recruit people who have a good background in teaching or nursing who can take an assignment at a foreign training college for a period. With the right background, you might find an opportunity to help an organization write its programs into program specifications that can later be translated into construction specifications and construction bid documents. Other development organizations that might have a more or less unilateral mission are those which recruit doctors for mission hospitals or clinics. If one has the correct background, they might find an opportunity to participate in a research effort with the Centers for Disease Control or a related contract organization. One organization I came across raises funds for renovations at remote schools and helps plan and manage the school upgrades. Other more or less unilaterally focused development organizations might do projects in a single country, e.g. the breeding of horses for work in high mountain terrain, micro credit and training for women's enterprises, or the development of small fisheries businesses.

One way a person might find an avenue of engagement could be through an organization which has a sister relationship with another organization in a development setting, e.g. a hospital, a text book distributor, a prescription drug manufacturer, or a church. It is important to keep in mind that many small development organizations work through local personnel. This has the advantage of training for sustainability, keeping costs reasonable, and strengthening communities. It provides training for local people and gives employment. Even so, there are often opportunities for expatriate counterparts who can be of teaching and mentoring assistance and who can manage matters that are extremely sensitive from a cultural point of view.

While there are many opportunities with small to medium sized organizations and while these opportunities can be very fulfilling, allowing one to do important, creative, and culturally challenging work, many of the opportunities in overseas development are with large organizations which become involved in sector wide initiatives, sometimes for an entire country. With this in mind, let us briefly look at steps taken by such organizations toward the design, development, implementation, management, and monitoring of project or program initiatives. It is useful for anyone intent on a career in international development to have familiarity with this. Knowing of the strenuous design steps that are employed gives one an appreciation of the serious and dedicated work that such organizations do. It signals the professionalism of such organizations and makes you realize that a great deal of thought goes into development projects and programs. An aspiring professional can be proud to work with the development organizations in the field.

In this kind of development initiative, there are likely to be several partners. The host country is (or should be) key to all decision making and movement. Often, a host country and a donor agency will start the process with discussions on needs and conditions.

(1) This may result in a *Country Paper* which is a broad study of all sectors within the country and which examines major challenges and opportunities, e.g. natural resources, human resources, education levels, health conditions, labor availability, soil, water, weather and minerals, challenges of governance, cultural conditions, migration, the existence of refugee populations, law and order, land tenure, population growth, etc. It provides a multi sector view of a country.

(2) Through this process, the identification of a sector for development work ensues. This results in a *Comprehensive Sector Assessment* which is a detailed study of one of the

economic sectors. For example, a sector assessment in the education sector might have the following sections: Executive Summary, Purpose of the Assessment, Methodology of the Assessment, Major Stages of the Assessment, System Overview (students, teachers, curriculum, standards, schools and facilities, governance, management, funding, and resources), Assessment of Access, Equity, Quality, Relevance, Learning Environment, Governance, Management, and recommended Policy Priorities for Improvement. The study would culminate with conclusions and recommended steps.

(3) Should the host government and the donor agency agree at this point, a *Project Identification Paper* would be commissioned. This identifies the problems and challenges to be addressed in the sector.

(4) Assuming that the Project Identification Paper is acceptable, the host country and donor agency will proceed with a *Project Paper* which is a comprehensive blueprint for work to be done within a specific time period. This is a critical guide consisting of (a) the development setting – with sections on the country and its people, education past and present, government policies and strategies, and employment (b) a project overview consisting of problem identification, project rationale, project description, project relationship to country development strategy, relationship of project to projects of other donors, cost implications, economic analysis, and socio/cultural analysis (c) project administration – consisting of sections on coordination, evaluation and monitoring, contracting considerations, and environmental considerations (d) annexes, e.g. technical assistance scopes of work, cost estimates, training plans, commodity and equipment lists, required approvals, social soundness analysis, statutory checklists and covenants agreed to on personnel, office space and policies.

(5) This is accompanied by a *Project Assistance Document* that spells out organizational and managerial matters between the host country and the donor agency.

(6) Based on this, a detailed *Request for Proposals (RFP)* is issued.

(7) Organizations that are qualified to manage a major and involved sector wide project are invited to submit a thorough *Project Proposal* by which they would accomplish the goals and objectives stated by the RFP.

(8) Further work before a project is initiated might include a *Best and Final Submission.*

(9) *A Logical Framework* which maps the entire project follows. This diagrams sector goals related to project purpose, intended outputs by magnitude, project assumptions and proposed actions related to intended progress, and means of verification. A detailed work plan is often submitted at this point.

Unless one is engaged in senior management within a development organization, or unless they regularly engage in research, design, and implementation consultancies, they will not need to be thoroughly acquainted with the above process.

However, having knowledge of the big picture and the overall process will make them more understanding of the work their specific role calls for and will give them an appreciation that there is a professional base to the work of their organization. Knowing the significant and interrelated problems that a project is attempting to address will breed pride in one's work. Development work is indeed substantive, challenging, and most worthwhile.

Chapter VI
Working in Education

What Might You Do if You Decide to Work in Education Development?

You could of course teach. That is at the core of education. However, there are a great many other things you could do. As the title of Chapter V says, "Development Opportunities Do Not Just Happen." Each is connected to a major problem or challenge in society. Given the complexity of societies and the serious problems that need attention, the range of development specialties seems almost endless. A major deficiency or catastrophe in society may require well-targeted initiatives by many development specialists. One particular challenge may become the focus of many types of expertise.

Developing Societies Are Different

The problems in developed societies may be much more discernible because they have been defined and categorized. The solutions and skills which need to be applied are usually readily identifiable. The developed world has solutions for problems that are predefined and have so called professionals who, through education and experience, have been qualified and certified to deal with them. The developing world is less boxed in, is more fluid, and perhaps more of a challenge to those who work in it. While it is important that those who work in development become grounded in a specialty through education and experience, it is also important that they be creative, having the energy and desire to re-shape themselves in relation to whatever challenge comes along. That goes with the nature of developing societies.

An Example

Allow me to share information about work in an education development project based on the needs of a country. The project was labeled "Basic and Non Formal Education Systems". Given this nation's difficult situation (rapidly expanding population, more and more landlessness, increasing unemployment, extremely limited resources, number of young people who never enroll in school, high student dropout rate for those who do enroll, the pressure for female children to stay at home and assist with domestic chores, e.g. carrying water for several miles each day, the need for boys and girls to stay away from school during long harvesting seasons, and poor achievement for those who do stay in school), *the overarching goal of the project can be summed up as: to help provide effective and relevant education in an equitable way to a quickly expanding population through initiatives that avoid expensive and unsustainable expansion of the conventional system.*

The Kingdom of Lesotho, formerly a British protectorate, is a constitutional monarchy, having gained its independence in 1966. It is a small mountainous and landlocked country, the only country in the world which is entirely 5000 feet or more above sea level. In geographic size it is similar to some of the modest in size US States. Only 13% the Kingdom of Lesotho's land is arable. Notwithstanding, agriculture is the main economic activity, employing about 66% of the labor force. There is considerable population pressure, overgrazing, and serious soil erosion. Over 90% of the population is rural. The nation's population is young with over 40% under the age of 15. The growing population continues to increase pressures on food production.

The driving force of Lesotho's economy from independence on has been income generated by sending workers abroad to work in South African mines. In fact, at the time of the project, some 75% of wage earners worked abroad in those mines. Remittances from people who were working abroad constituted 41% of GDP. However, it was known that this would one day diminish severely as a politically changed South Africa trained its own people to work in its mines. Lesotho's survival would depend on its ability to expand domestic employment opportunities and to shift from dependence on wage remittances. It would need to become much more self-reliant at home and eventually expand its export capacity. The proposed education reform initiative would place value on self-reliance and the acquisition of skills which could contribute to self-employment and national well-being.

The Nation's Education System

During colonial times Lesotho was considered a labor reserve for South Africa, requiring only basic schooling. Development of middle and high level manpower was not thought important. The nation became almost totally dependent on foreign nationals for skills requiring long term or sophisticated schooling. There are other countries with such an employment policy but for different reasons.

The nation did develop an extensive network of schools for basic education, many private, but some of them public, after independence. Formal education came to be seven years of primary and five years of secondary (i.e. three years of junior secondary and two years of senior secondary). University education was established in modest measure, formal teacher education was developed, and several vocational schools were established. Even so, economic pressures were such on young people that many did not remain in school very long or progress very far. There was the problem of lack of faith in the education system, which discouraged parents from investing too many years of their children's lives in formal schooling. It was not uncommon for primary teachers to have 80 and more students in their classes. A visitor to a school might walk several miles from the nearest road or trail head to find upon arrival that some students could not be accommodated inside the building and were seated on the ground outside the door. Many school facilities were very inadequate. Some 28% of enrolled students did not have a school with a substantial roof. Many did not have a table to write on. One third of primary teachers were classified as less than properly qualified. By the beginning of the seventh year of schooling, almost one half of those who had originally enrolled had left. The dropout rate meant that efficiency was such that for every child who did complete seven years of education, the government had paid for 14 years of schooling. However, the adult population did apparently feel the need for basic literacy. Non-formal education, for this purpose, became widespread. But it was obvious that schooling was failing the nation's people and was not functional in relation to needs. Students were not gaining the values, habits, understandings, and skills that would lead to productive wage employment or help them become self-employed. Much of the skilled work in the country (technical and managerial in both the private and public sectors) still had to be performed by foreign nationals.

Organized public dialogues throughout Lesotho led to the conclusion that education would have to be integrated into society much more relevantly and be able to address the people's practical needs. Three key goals emerged. They were the development of public education which would (1) provide quality basic education for all (2) more effectively link education, training, and work and (3) provide sufficient numbers of people with appropriate occupational, technical, and managerial skills to develop and operate a modern economy with modern public institutions.

The Education Reform Project

The nation with the help of recruited technical assistance designed, over time, a comprehensive education development project to address the goals noted above. It would turn out to necessitate a coordinated multifaceted approach. The nation's leaders came to recognize that each part of the nation's education system affects all others and that effective and relevant schooling would depend on a system that works together efficiently.

Hence the Basic and Non Formal Education Systems Project had provisions to upgrade and reform instruction at all levels through interventions at the schools and at all supporting institutions. It would address deficiencies in policy and policy coordination, research, training, curriculum and materials, teaching methods, testing, institutional management, personnel administration, financial operations, communications, facilities and furnishings, distributions and dissemination, parental and community support, and external NFE and adult literacy services. It was a project offering great opportunity and lasting benefit if the people would make it their own and if the nation's government could find innovative ways of continuing support for it.

The project would be implemented in a nation of several small cities and hundreds of villages, existing in great valleys surrounded by stately mountains. It was a place where dramatic poverty existed within a setting of great natural beauty, but also a place of gradual economic and social change.

The Approach

Several committees of the Ministry of Education and other bodies determined that interventions would be needed that could address four main problems:

A. Ineffectiveness of Basic Instruction at the Primary and Secondary Levels

B. Instructional Irrelevance to Socioeconomic Challenges

C. Inefficient Administration and Delivery of Education Services

D. Lack of Community Cohesiveness and Engagement with the Schools

An entire book could be written explaining the interventions put into place to address these four national challenges. However, allow me to provide brief notes related to each. And because the book you are reading is about choosing a career in international development, allow me to note some of the long and medium term development positions, or as called then technical assistance positions, that became a part of the project. Please remember that each of these would be appended to a local position of like nature, so that the international experts had local counterparts. The international advisors would one day leave. The local counterparts would of course, stay and have to carry on what had been put into place. The relationship between international advisors and local counterparts would determine the extent to which this would fall into place. So if you had been on the scene, what would have been the possible scopes of work available to you?

A. Ineffectiveness of Basic Instruction

1. SITUATION – high and increasing pupil to teacher ratio

An Intervention – undertaken by international advisors with local colleagues

Explanation – Resources would not allow a conventional approach to reducing the pupil to teacher ratio, i.e. the hiring of more teachers. Short cuts to effectively reduce the ratio were employed – including radio instruction, design and introduction of programmed instructional materials, the supply of teaching charts and other aids, and extensive methods training across the country through several models of delivery.

Imagine yourself doing this work*. Keep in mind that often in projects like this, a senior international advisor for an intervention doesn't just follow directions but rather is called upon to improve the basic design and manage the effort, which might have to do with conceptualizing the intervention, developing a strategy, detailing steps to be taken, getting an ok from project management, obtaining approval from the relevant national Ministry, thorough discussions with the donor or donors on behalf of the project, planning for the hiring and training of local staff that would be needed, coordination with institutions of the host country which would need to be involved, providing information to communities across the country on the initiative, signing up participants based on some sort of incentive (e.g. special credit, an increase in pay, the advantage of having new skills and materials, etc.), determining equipment, vehicles, perhaps horses, and other things that would be needed, determining the need for short term specialized help during the intervention, determining an implementation schedule and work plan by month, year, and multi years periods, complying with the law if that is relevant, making provision for accreditation of the systems to be put into place if that is relevant, overall supervision and evaluation, all consistent with project procedures and protocols. Keep in mind that all of this is done cross culturally which makes it more difficult but also much more interesting.*

Based on this explanation, what academic and experiential background would you wish to have in order to qualify for and satisfactorily carry out this intervention?

2. SITUATION – poor teacher qualifications

An Intervention – undertaken by international advisors with local colleagues

Explanation – Given the lack of capacity of formal teacher training in Lesotho, it would take many years to bring the teaching force of thousands up to standard through this avenue. Hence, a separate evening college for teachers was organized at several locations across the country. Also, a traveling teacher in-service education program was instituted for especially isolated teachers. In addition, the government inspectorate was trained to help teachers with special teaching challenges and teachers were given "methods" in-service instruction by radio. Also, a comprehensive upgrading of formal Teacher's College training was undertaken involving curriculum redesign, the development of new teaching materials, professional teacher training in country and abroad, and the upgrading of administrative and support systems.

Based on this short description and the general explanation of international advisor responsibilities in section A.1 above, imagine doing this work. What academic and experiential background would you find helpful?

3. SITUATION – inequitable and poor schooling conditions

An Intervention – undertaken by international advisors with local colleagues

Explanation – Because school construction and renovation would take many years, especially in the most remote regions where roads did not exist, the project found shortcuts, e.g. the making and introduction of thousands of lapboards as desks, community mobilization to repair schools, and training to help teachers make better use of existing schools. Such shortcuts were especially important because it was not uncommon for students in some locations to study in stone and thatch buildings with no heat, partial roofs, not enough chairs, no indoor bathrooms, no running water, and not enough space for all enrolled students to sit inside. It was common for teachers to take students outside on sunny days to warm up.

Based on this short description and the general explanation of international advisor responsibilities in section A.1 above, imagine yourself doing this work. What sort of academic and experiential background would you wish to have?

4. SITUATION – inadequate instructional materials

An Intervention – undertaken by international advisors with local colleagues

Explanation – Given the paucity of teaching and learning materials, the Project and Host Ministry developed teaching guides, textbooks and resource materials in math, reading, science, agriculture, home economics, business studies, health and nutrition, together with exercise books, charts, games, workbooks, garden tools, monthly student magazines, and professional journals for teachers. These were regularly produced and disseminated across the country together with instruction and practice for teachers on their use.

Based on this short description and the general explanation of international advisor responsibilities in section A.1 above, imagine yourself doing this work. What academic and experiential background would you find helpful?

5. SITUATION – inequitable and inefficient distribution of school materials

An Intervention – undertaken by international advisors and local colleagues

Explanation – given the unevenness of supplies, guides, teaching aids, announcements, school calendars, test information and alerts, school to school and region to region, reorganization and upgrading of the national school supply unit in terms of publishing, management, and accounting was initiated. A national dissemination unit was organized to give workshops and issue materials throughout the country. Dissemination networks of teachers were organized cascade style, whereby groups would come together by discipline and schedule for discussions of new materials and methods. The place of meeting would also be the pickup location for school supplies.

Based on this brief description and the explanation of international advisor responsibilities in Section A.1 above, imagine yourself doing this work. What academic and experiential background would you wish to have?

6. SITUATION – inadequate student diagnosis and testing – hence inappropriate student placement, grouping, pacing, instruction and performance.

An Intervention – undertaken by international advisors and local colleagues

Explanation – given the disadvantages of students who had teachers lacking in appropriate knowledge, skills, and materials, nationwide teacher training on skills, objective setting, lesson planning, observation, evaluation, diagnostic exercises, end of level testing, and other methods of assessment was carried out.

Based on this brief description and the explanation of international advisor responsibilities in Section A.1 above, imagine yourself doing this work. What academic and experiential background would you wish to have?

7. SITUATION – inadequate second chance opportunities

An intervention – undertaken by international advisors and local colleagues

Explanation – given that so many people in the country had either not attended school or had dropped out in the earliest grades and hence not retained what they had learned, the establishment of a community learning system, i.e. a model literacy and numeracy program, was undertaken using trained volunteer tutors throughout the country, with specially developed programmed materials.

Based on this brief description and the explanation of international advisor responsibilities in Section A.1 above, imagine doing this work. What academic and experiential background would you find helpful?

B. Instructional Irrelevance to National Socioeconomic Challenges and Needs

8. SITUATION – The country's academic curriculum, taught very traditionally and at the lowest level of the cognitive hierarchy, was not integrated, not applied, and not used for problem solving. There was an inadvertent discrediting of rural life and of occupational and entrepreneurial skills and understandings.

An intervention – undertaken by international advisors and local colleagues

Explanation – Because of the disconnect between traditional schooling and everyday life, the project developed and disseminated resource directories, tools, and case studies. It also instructed teachers on applied learning whereby classroom teaching was immediately used to solve practical village problems and became an instrument for economic thinking. The project initiated school farming tied to the sciences and other parts of the curriculum and established a model rural skills training school, high in the remote mountains, which had capacity for self-support through economic activities.

Based on this brief description and the explanation of international advisor responsibilities in section A.1 above, imagine doing this work. What academic and experiential background would you like to have?

C. Inefficient Delivery of Education Services

9. SITUATION – Unclear policies and lack of priorities in the education system

An intervention – undertaken by international advisors and local colleagues.

Explanation – because of the lack of clarity on education philosophy, strategies, and policies, the project worked with the Ministry of Education and schools (both public and private) on participatory policy clarification through meetings and conferences and helped develop annual operating plans for components of the Ministry.

Based on this brief description and the explanation of international advisor responsibilities in Section A.1 above, imagine doing this work. What academic and experiential background would you wish to have?

10. SITUATION – Lack of organizational teamwork and coordinated performance

An intervention – undertaken by international advisors and local colleagues

Explanation – Given the need for an improved understanding of roles and responsibilities, organizational team work, initiative, performance management, and position accountability, the Project and Ministry of Education facilitated unit and individual work planning for components and institutions. This was coordinated with the participatory development of schemes of service for each unit and office. The Project and Ministry, and its many institutions, also developed position descriptions through participant workshops. Formalized institutional reporting was also introduced.

Based on this brief description and the explanation of international advisor responsibilities in section A.1 above, imagine doing this work. What academic and experiential background would you find helpful?

11. SITUATION – Inability to keep track of and control the human establishment, i.e. hire, monitor, evaluate, promote and pay consistently at Ministry offices, and service institutions throughout the system.

An Intervention – undertaken by international advisors and local colleagues

Explanation – given the problems this caused in terms of fairness, morale, performance, and budgeting, the Project and Ministry undertook a giant effort to update and computerize personnel records and functions throughout the entire national system, i.e. the Ministry of Education planning, administrative, financial and supervisory offices, and the national education service institutions, e.g. teacher education, curriculum development, testing and research, materials development, distance education techniques and methods, the inspectorate, non-formal education organizations, the university, university extension centers, etc.

Based on this brief description and the explanation of international advisor responsibilities in Section A.1 above, imagine doing this work. What academic and experiential background would you wish to have?

12. SITUATION – Undependable and inequitable supply to schools

Intervention – undertaken by international advisors and local colleagues

Explanation – Given this situation, the Project and Ministry of Education undertook the establishment of inventories, new planning and accounting systems, updated warehousing, improved transport, and creative dissemination to the thousands of schools.

Based on this brief description and the explanation of international advisor responsibilities in Section A.1 above, imagine yourself doing this work. What academic and experiential background would you wish to have?

13. SITUATION – An unorganized teacher personnel system

Intervention – undertaken by international advisors and local colleagues

Explanation – Given this situation, the Ministry of Education, with project assistance, undertook establishment of a teacher inventory system, computerized teacher work, and qualification records, upgraded payment and distribution systems, trained administrative staff on ways to make use of teacher personnel data to improve management and improved on budgeting and outreach.

Based on this brief description and the explanation on international advisor responsibilities in Section A.1 above, <u>imagine doing this work</u>. What academic and experiential background would you like to have?

14. SITUATION – Subjective policy development and decision making

Intervention – undertaken by international advisors and local colleagues

Explanation – Management across the system was tightly coupled, i.e. the organization was hierarchy driven although informally flat in some instances. Even so, control was loose. Realizing it was overly subject to the anarchy that arises from a steep hierarchy within, where employees do not have a chance to internalize, and where influential outside groups (political parties, church denominations, business interests, and others) are better informed than some elements of government, the Ministry of Education used project personnel and resources to thoroughly revamp its' management information. In addition to establishing an Education Management Information System for routine record keeping and planning, MIS data was regularly used to prepare for and support discussions, position paper development, policy development, and public relations.

Based on this brief description and the explanation of international advisor responsibilities in section A.1 above, <u>imagine yourself doing this work</u>. What academic and experiential background would you like to have?

15. SITUATION – Antiquated bookkeeping and budgeting

Intervention – undertaken by international advisors and local colleagues

Explanation – Given this situation, project advisors with local colleagues organized appropriate training for business officers of Ministry offices, service institutions, and field offices. The training was carried out within the country and abroad. A sister effort by project personnel and local colleagues undertook to decentralize budgeting with accountability throughout the system.

Based on this brief description and the explanation of international advisor responsibilities in Section A.1 above, imagine yourself doing this work. What academic and experiential background would you find helpful?

16. SITUATION – Poorly qualified administrative, supervisory, and teaching personnel

Intervention – undertaken by international advisors and local colleagues

Explanation – Given this situation, the Project together with the Ministry of Education carefully analyzed individual strengths and compared them with position needs. Based on findings, the project organized overseas training, regional study tours, in-country courses, and on the job skill development activities. Hundreds of trainings were designed, organized, carried out, and evaluated.

Based on this brief description and international advisor responsibilities as described in Section A. 1 above, imagine yourself doing this work. What academic and experiential background would you find helpful?

D. Lack of Community Cohesiveness Related to Education and Therefore Lack of Support and Engagement

17. SITUATION – Historically, communities and parents had not believed education was their business. The education establishment, although extremely modest, was beyond the average person's sphere of interest. This, in part, was no doubt because a large part of the population had no formal schooling and many others had very little.

Intervention – undertaken by international advisors and local colleagues

Explanation – Given this situation, the Project in cooperation with the Ministry, instituted community level action research to explicate school needs, engage local citizens in school issues, and development improvement plans and to pull parents and other community members together into PTA type activities. To the largest possible extent, communities were engaged to work towards local solutions to school challenges.

Based on this brief description and the explanation of international advisor responsibilities described in Section A.1 above, <u>imagine doing this work</u>. What academic and experiential background would you find helpful?

18. SITUATION – Separation of schools from their communities. Teachers were unsure if they should involve parents and unsure how to approach involvement in any case. Teachers, like other authority figures, were not to be questioned. Hidden cultural inhibitors made parental involvement difficult.

Intervention – undertaken by international advisors and local colleagues.

Explanation – Given this situation, the Project with the National Teacher Training College established seed schools throughout the country that would become models of enhanced teaching but also models of work with their communities and parents. Under guidance of the National Teacher Training College, joint school and community improvement plans and innovative school programs were created and implemented. These became models for other schools which were seeded to them by the National Teacher Training College and the Project. The Project and National Teacher Training College were also responsible for other programs, e.g. improved soil and water conservation teaching, better teaching about crop and vegetable production, improved teaching about animal production and horticulture, and the seeding of teaching methods that would integrate the school with the farms and businesses of their setting. As a part of the Project's cooperation with the National Teacher Training College, a major operations management improvement initiative was carried out at the college. This kind of effort was also undertaken at each of the other education service institutions in the country.

The Project worked closely with the National Teacher Training College in leading the schools to new ways of doing things. However, this effort was not limited to the Teacher Training College. Guidance and innovation at the schools was promoted by the Project through the Evening College, the Project National Dissemination Network, the Primary Teacher In-Service Education Program, the Adult Literacy Program, the Distance Education Center, the National Curriculum Development Center, the Institute of Extra Mural Studies, the National University, and the National Instructional Materials Resource Center. Without going into detail let me briefly note just five of the model programs. *The Project Development Communications Initiative* created radio programs with local actors on school and community development issues, *The Project Continuous Assessment Program* developed standard formats and protocols for continuous assessment at several grade levels, with the intent of improving methods and curricula in every aspect of schooling, *the National Educational Library Service Project* developed and acquired books, materials, photos, audiovisual presentations and radio broadcasts for the edification of teachers nationwide, *the Project English in Action Program* used radio as a tool to help teachers who wished to improve their facility with English and *The Project Small Business Studies Program* worked in several ways to help teachers better link classroom teaching with successful commercial employment for students upon finishing school.

Based on this description and the explanation of international advisor responsibilities in Section A.1 above, <u>imagine doing this work</u>. What education and work experience background would be helpful to you?

IMPORTANCE OF THE SETTING TO THOSE WHO WORK IN DEVELOPMENT

The idea of this book is to help you understand the issues and the work with which an advisor in international development is confronted. It is to help you see international development from the broader perspective than the technical. It is also to help you understand how challenging and exciting this work is, if done with caring dedication and professionalism. Finally, it is to give you an appreciation of how important down to earth international development is.

There is a wide range of conditions across the developing world. People and their ways and living situations differ dramatically from country to country. Some of the differences, society to society, are based on deep and long standing cultural history. Others are a function of the overall availability of resources. Some are a function of the distribution of resources or even more startling, the distribution of opportunity. Some are the offshoot of entrenched political power. Occasionally the difference might be based on a quiet struggle between civic and religious power. Developing societies, whether on the islands in one of the oceans, or on any of the continents, may on the surface give the appearance of either poverty or relative well-being. In some, a form of caste may still be controlling, even though illegal now. In others, the family name may mean everything. In others still, people are born into the exact position they will have for life. There are those where unemployment is extremely high even though the country is rich in resources and produces abundantly. There are others where young men have everything but are unhappy because they consider much of what they might do for a living as beneath them. There are those where privileged and highly educated young women are unable to contribute to the nation's economy except surreptitiously. In some of the poorest, there is something thought of as legitimate thievery because it is right to steal for one's children if they may otherwise starve. There are countries where a certain group controls civil service appointments across all Ministries, thus having great influence and wealth. There are others where it is customary for CEO's and senior politicians to use civil service manpower in their private businesses. In some, liberated and less than liberated women may be in a quiet struggle with each other for influence over customs. And there are some where those outside the social structure entirely, seem the happiest, although admittedly the happiness of the very poor and disenfranchised is difficult to truly assess. It is hard to imagine that the barefoot elderly tea boy who resides in the office closet of a powerful dignitary is always happy. The factors behind development and underdevelopment are many and complicated.

This being said, let us refer to the situation of the resource poor country where the project described above operated.

This is not to ascribe that country's situation to anything other than its poverty although one could do further analysis. The description which follows is meant to highlight the importance of "real world development". Every setting is different and International Development Advisors must come to understand any to which they are assigned, if they are to be successful. Genuine and caring interest in one's hosts and their situation is critical to success in our work.

A Picture of the General Situation

The picture below is based on general conditions in the country although details are not exact. They are presented to give a sense of the constraints under which the education system of this country functioned at the time of the project.

The Deputy Minister of Education who is responsible for all schools in this developing country typically arrives at his or her modestly appointed office to find people lined up. The issues of a typical day might include (a) a remote school has burned and parents feel they must speak with the Deputy Minister (b) a Ministry vehicle is missing from the Government lot and the Deputy Minister has to speak with the police (c) students in a remote village (four hours from the nearest dirt highway) have been refusing to attend school for two weeks because their teacher is said to have a serious drinking problem (d) the chairman of the committee on crediting teachers for courses taken has not shown up; his committee has waited two hours and are disgruntled. The Deputy Minister knows the chairman is making a statement through this action because Treasury has not paid him in over six months (e) there is no oil for the one smoky little heater that sits in the middle of the Deputy Minister's room. Being no heat, it is too cold to put pen to paper. The Deputy Minister's secretary, who would normally order oil, has had a death in the family; she will be out for a minimum of two weeks. The Deputy Minister will himself spend several hours on at least two occasions visiting his secretary's family and will spend an entire day at a tent funeral in her ancestral village, some nine hours away by 4-wheel drive vehicle and horseback. Incidentally, he will attend at least one full-day funeral every week.

There is no one else to take care of the heater. The Deputy Minister has a very small cadre of central office staff to handle an entire country. There is his Chief Education Officer, who is responsible for all academic programs at the University, the National Teacher Training College, the Agricultural College, the ten vocational schools and the Central Polytechnic. In addition, he or she is responsible for the Curriculum Development Centre, the Materials Development Centre, the Teacher Services Commission, and for liaison with the Church Education Secretariats. The Chief Education Officer usually gets around town on foot. For up-country trips he takes a small, overcrowded commercial bus. A combination of poor maintenance and belt-tightening under financial restructuring has left the Ministry with only two working vehicles out of its normal fleet of fifteen. The Chief Education Officer has a secretary. However, on days that she wears her best dress, some work is out of the question. A good dress is a very expensive item. There is the Deputy Minister's Executive Assistant who is responsible for all school finances, the government's books on school properties, school supplies, the maintenance of vehicles, and for construction. That is it. That is the complement of senior Ministry staff for the nation.

There are some middle level officers. For example, there are nineteen inspectors who have 4,500 schools to look after. In addition to supervision, the inspectors spend four months of each year grading government school exams. That's why there are remote schools which have not been visited yet this year.

There is a Ministry of Education Personnel Officer, but he has no help. Personnel records for the Ministry and its institutions (other than the schools) are with the National Civil Service Commission. The Personnel Officer hears complaints, attends meetings, and struggles to get the Civil Service Commission to act on vacancies, promotions, and like matters. Usually he fails. Letters go unanswered and phone calls are not returned. Of course, when he walks over to Civil Service Commission offices, everyone is pleasant to him. He is promised action, but it is not forthcoming because (a) Civil Service records are inaccessibly scattered in stacks of folders on the three floors of a leaky building, and (b) the government has secretly given the signal not to promote anyone, not to fill empty posts, and not to worry about back pay claims. They have little choice; they are practically broke. Incidentally, it is not uncommon for someone to suddenly drop out of work because they have not had a pay check in six months. A much more routine thing is that people keep their jobs but simply stop working. There are no other jobs to go to anyway.

There are other matters before the Deputy Minister today – the Canadians are coming by at 9:30, the EEC will be in at 11:00, and representatives of the Mennonite Central Committee will come by after lunch. The Deputy Minister will politely say yes to all of the conditions attached to the contribution these people offer. For the university dormitory that the Canadians will build, the Deputy Minister will pledge upkeep staff, a maintenance budget, and the provision of utilities. Failure to do this will come to a head with university students long after the Canadians have gone on to something else. For the vocational school that the EEC will build, the Deputy Minister will promise to pay staff salaries and other operational costs beginning in year five. Of course, this cannot really happen. His government will try hard to get another donor to do it.

For the health education packages that the Mennonites provide, the Deputy Minister will promise to schedule time in the weekly school calendar for health instruction. His government can of course do this, but it will make little difference. Public school hours are 9:30 to 3:00, but many children walk for two hours. Therefore, they are very often late and they are tired. In winter months, it is not uncommon for a teacher to begin classes at 11: OO a.m. There are no desks for over one-third of the nation's students. On winter days, they go outside to be in the warm sun. And when youngsters are inside, conditions are so crowded that many instructional activities are precluded. Inside the old stone, windowless buildings it is cold and dark. Much of the short school day is given over to singing to keep bodies warm and spirits up. There is no cafeteria and no gym. Kids begin walking home in the early afternoon. They used to stay longer but the World Food Program was cut. It was said that after 25 years of school lunches (flour and bread), the nation was too dependent. It could not feed its children because of the disincentive of the handouts. So, the Deputy Minister cannot really guarantee there will be a weekly time when the Mennonite health kits will be used. Indeed, he cannot guarantee there will be a time during the week when reading, writing, or math will be taught.

He certainly cannot guarantee the distribution of the health kits. And it is unfortunate that for those kits which do get through to remote schools, many teachers (who have less than a full secondary education themselves) will not understand how to use them. If there is wood in the kits, a few desperate schools may use some of it for heat on especially damp days. That is if the kits get delivered to remote sites in the first place. When the government post and transport service is overly loaded, it quietly discards things.

Let's see...other issues that the Deputy Minister will be confronted with today...the cardboard patch in one of his windows has fallen out and a power outage is happening...oh, well, that's no issue at all. It happens almost every day. It only affects people in the capitol city. Ninety-five percent of the Deputy Minister's schools have no electricity to begin with. There are the 27 computers placed in education service institutions around town by donors. Some are with the Teacher Service Commission, some at the Teachers College, some at the Materials Development Centre, and some are at the Curriculum Centre. But because the project that placed them left, they have fallen out of use one-by-one; no repair monies and no one to handle serious servicing. The Deputy Minister is briefly reminded of the problem his remote schools have had in getting replacement batteries for radios that are used to receive special school broadcasts.

Bothering the Deputy Minister more than anything this morning is the delegation that will come in from the Roman Catholic Bishop's office. As it happens, the Deputy Minister is Catholic. His government staggers appointments – a Catholic, then an Evangelical, and then an Anglican. He will feel a special pressure from this group. They will want a new school opened in a growing village. He has no money for teachers. They (the Church) are starting to build the school already. The people are behind them. But location and size are contrary to the World Bank sponsored mapping plan that Government has promised to follow. Still, the Deputy Minister does not want to get on the wrong side of the Church. It would look especially bad at the moment. Church newspapers and certain members of Government are at each other's throats over social issues. Five clergymen have mysteriously died in their sleep in the last few months which heightens paranoia, although there is no proof of illicit cause. Protestants and Catholics are being set against each other again. There is rumor that food poisonings in villages are once again gaining ground, although it is still rare. But even in the capitol, there have been one or two recent instances of civil servants being quietly poisoned by someone. No, the Deputy Minister must play this one very carefully. When it comes to the country's churches, political factions, old families, clans, and certain villages, his negotiations can have life and death consequences.

I could go on and on about the matters that the Ministry of Education has to deal with from day-to-day. There are so many more angles and demands that are strange to us. They are just the conditions of a very poor country. So for example, while out of courtesy a hard-pressed developing country may agree with a rich donor to facilitate "policy-related research", in reality they perhaps do not see how it is related to their problems.

It is important to note that with all of the Ministry's problems, its officers remain unwaveringly civil, polite, and accommodating. As poor as they are and as pressed as they are by financial restructuring obligations, even though they may be slipping further and further behind in meeting the needs of an ever increasing population, the people of this, and I believe many developing countries, have an unwritten civility code, a togetherness; a time for people that many of us in the so-called developed world have lost. There is certainly much less emphasis on individual competitiveness. People share whatever they have, however little it may be. There may be lots of poor people on the streets, but they are usually not homeless. The extended family looks out for unwed mothers, for distant cousins, for the very elderly, for those who have crossed the law, for those without work, and for fathers who just cannot feed their children. People are loyal to kin no matter how distant. What one has belongs to the family, and to a slightly less extent, to the village. The concept of ownership is different from ours. People's values are not nearly as materially-based as those of the West. What is mine also belongs to you if you are in need.

In the much of the developing world, it seems as if people are more important than institutions. Hence the necessity of our learning to get things done through a personal local network in addition to the western bureaucracy of which we are a part. Senior civil servants in developing countries have come to learn they must take seriously the things that are laid on by donors but in reality for example, there is no urgency about dealing with a piece of paper, except that the donor or development partner expects it. People in the developing world like to talk things through. They have occasions for this, a two day funeral, for example. But they will only really get down to in-depth talk with an outsider if he or she has been amongst them for some time, if he or she has won their confidence, if he or she is known to be sincerely interested in problems as they see them, and if he or she has worked side-by-side with them on the types of things described above, i.e. the types of thing a Deputy Minister of Education faces upon entering his office in the morning. Even technically poor interventions work in the rare instance where a long-standing and deep relationship is in place. Where that has not been established, the very best of donor interventions fail.

People in the region of the above project still savor the moment. It is still alright to be quiet and still, to savor life, to revel in a feeling, to be content with what is, to be happy with now, and whatever will be. It is still alright in much of the third world to be gentle and to be unpretentious. There is not a great need to appear clever. Simple greetings and broad smiles come easily even in the face of extreme hardship. It is okay that one does not have the latest technique, the latest gadget, or the latest fashion. It is okay that one has not seen the latest movie or been party to the latest cause. Purpose to people in the developing world can be something very different from purpose in so called advanced nations. Still though, the most sophisticated of local leaders straddle developed and developing ways of doing things because they appreciate the results. We too, as development specialists, need to learn to straddle the two worlds of our work because we have respect for others and because we realize this is necessary if we are to be successful.

Things like time, human organization, the sources of wisdom, the transfer of knowledge, decision making, delegation, action, reporting back, and accountability are very different in our two worlds. A sophisticated leader from the developing world understands that in the post industrialized world, society is organized such that orderly step by step change can be brought about through the rational application of findings. He or she also knows how very different his or her world is. We too need to appreciate how different our world is from his or hers and we need to understand how to work through both.

I know from experience that we can help people in developing countries take hold of their dilemmas and bring about needed change. To do so, we need to stand back a bit and support local people as they work on critical agendas, the culturally complex and politically sensitive agendas that we do not see.

EXAMPLES OF OTHER ASSIGNMENTS FOR SPECIALISTS IN EDUCATION

1. Teach English as a foreign language in a secondary school of a South Asian city.

2. Develop a plan of methods training for the teachers of a remote school in East Africa. The school has 470 students in grades one through six. Base the plan on grade levels, the required national curriculum, and program options desired by the community. Also base the plan on teacher needs and community research. Include ideas on teacher developed instructional materials and on administrator training. Present the plan and if accepted, carry out the proposed training over the period of eighteen months by teaching units of instruction and by using recruited short term specialists.

3. Develop a long range plan for education extension services in a developing country in southern Africa. Include local partners from institutions of learning in this and with them, develop and agree to a comprehensive philosophy of extension education for the nation, an institutional

management philosophy, a teaching program to be delivered by extension, a guide on procedures for community research in support of the program, a plan of community outreach, a staffing plan consistent with the proposed academic, research, and outreach programs, a long range organizational plan, educational specifications for a new central campus and several field campuses, a staff recruitment and training plan, and an estimated operational budget for each the first five years of operation.

4. Help local officials develop a long range plan to reorganize and upgrade a provincial education system in an East Asian country. Advise the chairman of a Provincial Planning Board consisting of representatives from the Provincial Board of Education, a Provincial University, an area Technical College, the Provincial Teachers Association, the Provincial Federation of School Parents, the Association of School Boards, and the Provincial Chamber of Commerce. Advise the local Coordinator of Regional Boards that will submit recommendations to the Provincial Planning Board. Assist the Chairman of the Provincial Board and his staff to prepare and submit proposals to the Provincial Cabinet. Planning will include the consolidation of school districts, the expansion and refinement of programs of instruction in relation to projected economic and social changes in the province, new formulas for school operational funding, and a sequenced plan of school construction in the growth areas of the province.

5. Participate on an international team, consisting of both local educators and expatriate advisors, to research and recommend comprehensive reforms for the education system of a country in East Asia. The work will include comparative research on the features, practices and approach to change of the world's most successful education systems, the implementation of a national assessment of education in the host country, the development of a national vision for education,

development of a national strategic plan for education, a plan for institutional and agency discussion of recommendations, a plan of public education on proposed changes, and a participatory plan for regional and national implementation.

6. Manage short term observation research in a select group of schools in a country of Central Asia to measure the effectiveness of instruction. The observation research will be grounded on a recognized model of effectiveness. Responsibilities will include training of researchers on instruments of observation, the selection of schools for the study in accordance with recognized sampling methods, and coordination with the National Ministry of Education, District Offices of Education and the selected schools. Responsibilities will also include the scheduling of all work, logistics coordination, supervision of the analysis of findings and the writing of initial reports.

7. Lead a team consisting of host country nationals and international advisors to assess the preparedness and capacity of government departments and institutions in a South Asian country, to take actions intended under a five year multi-million dollar education development project. Each of forty seven proposed major reforms will require an appropriate and secure foundation. The assessment will include on site studies of organizational structure, policies and practices, a review of management approaches, a review of positions, vacancies and ability to fill vacancies, interviews of senior and middle level personnel across the system, and discussion with appropriate community leaders to determine capacity and commitment. The work will include a formal report on readiness with suggestions of remedial actions needed prior to implementation of the proposed project.

8. Lead a team that will prepare a proposal for a national education project in a Near Eastern country. The proposal

will outline project assistance to the host country government and its institutions in the matter of extending pre-school education across the nation. This will include plans for curriculum development, facility development, the establishment of pre-school teacher training, and a plan to recruit and contract teachers, supervisors, and administrators. It will also propose development of a model for the rolling accreditation of participating schools. The proposal will address the management of pre-school education across the nation and provide insights on local and national budgeting for the system. It will also address parental engagement and school level organization. The proposal will explain how the project will assist the host government in the development of national education policy relevant to management of national pre-school education.

9. Lead a team that will prepare a proposal for a national education project in a South American country. The proposal will outline project assistance to a host country government and its institutions in the matter of extending youth and workforce training across the nation. The proposal will speak to ICT based curriculum development, facility and equipment development, both pre-service and in-service teacher training, accreditation systems, and a transition program for school to work in grades 9-12. The project proposal will also speak to assistance in development of policy appropriate to implementation and management.

10. Lead a team that will study the adequacy and relevance of education in an African nation to a port city's manpower needs in an evolving special economic zone. Responsibilities will include interviews with officials of the Ministry of Education, education managers, supervisors of teachers in the free trade zone – business, community and professional leaders, current employees, and aspiring youth. The work will culminate in the design of

interventions in education relevant to present and anticipated social and economic needs.

11. Conduct on site research in Central America to generate findings on a project's organization, management, field operations, staff relationships, and professional reputation with Ministry offices, institutional personnel, and community leaders. Make team building recommendations to the project's home office and if approved, organize to carry them out.

12. Lead a team of international advisors and host country professionals to construct a sub-sector program to a five year public education development project in West Africa. The work will require establishment of a capacity building and institutional development plan for all agency offices and institutions of the national public school system.

13. Lead a project team on national school monitoring and evaluation in South Asia. The National School Monitoring and Evaluation Project will develop a system to monitor all aspects of public education across the nation's 84,000 schools. A part of the system will evaluate achievement against system-wide and school/community input and process factors. In addition the project will conduct cost benefit studies, school management and leadership studies, and community involvement analyses. The main focus of the effort will be classroom organization and methods of instruction. A chief focus will also be generation of relevant information and procedures for information systems development and institutional capacity building.

14. Serve as Headmaster of a private (NGO supported) school for disadvantaged pupils in a remote mountainous region of Latin America. The school has 900 pupils in grades 1 to 12. The Headmaster has jurisdiction over every aspect of the school, i.e. academic, materials and equipment, business management and development,

teacher recruitment, supervision and upgrading, student counseling, parental engagement, community relations, and school to government coordination. The Headmaster will work with an international Board of Directors and a community based Home and School Association.

15. Serve as Director of an international Basic Education and Literacy project. The project is designed to work as needed in any location of the developing world. It is meant to improve the efficiency with which basic education and/or literacy is delivered, the quality of basic education and/or literacy, and access to and participation in basic education and literacy. The project will work at three levels, i.e. (1) the policy level where resource priorities are set (2) the service institution level and (3) the school level. The project will (a) facilitate applied research and demonstration pilots that are requested (b) organize needed technical assistance (C) conduct training. It is meant to work in any developing country that applies for assistance and that is approved by the donor group. The Director will supervise every project function, engage daily in staff and client development, engage in the design of initiatives that will meet client needs, and participate in training.

16. Serve as Chief of Party for a nationwide education development project. The project has initially been funded for five years. The Chief of Party will be in charge of international advisors who have been employed to help host country professionals (1) expand access to education through curriculum reform, materials development, and teacher training (2) link education to practical work and living skills (3) increase community support for and involvement in education (4) promote community based vocational and entrepreneurial education (5) integrate various operations into a single coherent national system of education (6) improve operations at several national institutions and (7) expand literacy opportunities to out of school youth and adults. The Chief of Party will supervise

personnel who design and operationalize special initiatives in literacy instruction, community development, materials development, equipment acquisition, radio and other distance teaching, formal teacher education, in-service teacher education, organizational development in non-formal education, and development of a remote vocational education and community school. The Chief of Party will work closely with host country Ministry of Education officials, officials of other Ministries, the heads of national institutions, the prime contract institution, and seven sub-contract institutions. He or she will also work closely with the donor agency.

17. Consult over a period of eight months with local and national educators in a war torn nation to develop a plan of action for a contracted education development organization. The education system in this country has been devastated by more than two decades of war. As a result, the majority of children and youth have little or no education. The number of over-aged, uneducated children and youth is in the millions. However, with the end of hostilities, unprecedented numbers of students of all ages wish to return to school, either to traditional school or to some sort of schooling of a non-formal or distance nature. Previous restrictive access to schooling, especially for girls, has resulted in a severe imbalance with approximately half of enrolled students in the first grade. Mixed grade and age classrooms are the norm with many primary students several years older than would ordinarily be the case. Because the school system was so devastated by war, huge numbers of children remain outside because the system does not have teaching or facility capacity. Many others remain on the outside because they have reached an age when they have to assume adult work responsibilities. Responding to this situation and these needs, the newly constituted national government has declared a policy of rehabilitation with access for all as an ultimate goal. The government has identified several key areas of immediate

need. They are: rehabilitation of existing buildings, construction of new buildings, the upgrading of teacher skills, the recruitment and training of new teachers, the provision of teaching materials, the revision of curriculum such that schooling equips students for living and working, provision of functional literacy, accelerated learning for out of school youth, and the provision of vocational opportunities for students with no access to basic education. Consistent with these urgent needs, the government and a major donor nation have agreed to address the most critical problems through a targeted development project of four components, i.e. (1) text book writing and production (2) radio based teacher training (both pre-service and in-service) (3) accelerated learning to bring over aged students up to grade level in as short a period as possible (4) technical assistance to government to bring about national education policy reform and development related to the challenges identified here through widespread dialogue. These initiatives will need to be carried out in regions where peace is not yet fully in place and where resources have been drained to almost nothing. The position will be one of developing detailed plans for these initiatives in full cooperation with national and local education leaders.

18. Serve as Team Leader of a project designed to increase the capacity of a university in an African nation. The project is designed to increase the capacity of the university to extend functional education to adults in an applied way, throughout a remote region. Objectives of the project include increasing extension enrollments, planning for expansion of education to un-served areas, improving articulation among extension divisions in the interest of program quality and efficiency, upgrading administrative and supervisory practices, developing new part-time programs of instruction for working adults, improving planning and budgeting, putting a management information system in place, improving capacity for

meaningful and credible needs research, improving proposal writing capability, re-organizing small business training programs, introducing a diploma in adult education for extension personnel, upgrading broadcast and journalism capacity, and improving the ability of designated university staff to carry out community development projects. The project will work closely with the university on facility construction and the hiring and training of new staff. It will also work closely with the university on the improvement of departmental abilities in community and development research, academic planning, part time studies organization, curriculum and program development, and public relations. The project will assist the university with area conferences that introduce part-time studies for working adults of a functional nature that employ both theoretical and applied methods.

19. Serve on the Quality Review Panel of a major financing institution. The panel will study a multi-donor proposal on a nationwide program of reform and development for education in a South Asian country. Information and research will be generated from interviews in the host country, study of the proposal with supporting documents, and meetings at institution headquarters in Washington D.C. The development program, not to be confused with a development project, will be, if approved, carried out over a period of five years. In brief, the panel will do an analysis of the proposed sector-wide program in terms of strengths and limitations (e.g. degree to which it is donor and time driven, degree to which it addresses the tough issues, is strategic, is appropriately prioritized, and has adequate implementation arrangements). The panel will also analyze program elements in relation to government ownership of the program, preparation of the participating donors, extent to which host government weaknesses may be exacerbated by program structure, and extent to which donors are aligned on investments, actions, desired behavioral changes, and outcomes. The panel will also

examine provisions for donor transparency, options for the structuring of funding and dispersal, adequacy of proposed budget support, monitoring and evaluation, and coverage of proposed interventions. In addition, the panel will study host country readiness and capacity to implement, manage, and sustain, i.e. readiness to make necessary changes in personnel practices, readiness of its various divisions to engage in the program effectively, and readiness of its divisions regarding planning and decision making.

20. Serve as Team Member on a project that will employ specific interventions in education to address the need for income generation and conflict mitigation. The project will work in a country where long standing and unfortunate social conditions festered into a violent civil war, which has after an extended time, come to an unsteady end. It is hoped that peace will gradually open the door for humanitarian relief and the beginning of development initiatives that will rebuild confidence, family cohesiveness, community cooperation, government services, national infrastructure, business, and employment. Peace will not automatically eliminate lingering grievances. Without the skillful repair of fundamental conditions, things will eventually come apart again or at least not work very well. The end of war in this unfortunate nation will leave social marginalization, economic disparity, gender discrimination, illiteracy, disease, landlessness, malnourishment, orphan-hood, and homelessness in place. Some of this was there before the war and some was added by the war. In some way, the fear and distrust that grew when both sides of the conflict were practicing property destruction, kidnapping, killing, torture, and detention will need to be addressed if neighbors, who were on competing sides, will ever be able to live together again and if communities will be able to work together again. Displaced people and alienated communities will need to be brought together as central to the re-development of the country. Otherwise development accomplishments will be shallow,

partial, and temporary. Project personnel will need to work shoulder to shoulder with local people as they become ready. It is anticipated that the abundance of cynicism, fear, and fatalism brought about by war will be overcome as project personnel demonstrate trust and respect for local partners and bring people of different groups together for project activities.

The project will work to mitigate conflict by training targeted youth for employment. It will have distinct but cooperating initiatives i.e. (a) improving literacy, life skills, and peace building skills for targeted youth (b) increasing vocational training and employment opportunities for targeted youth (c) increasing rural incomes and agriculture productivity for targeted youth and (d) providing scholarships to targeted youth.

THE HUMAN SIDE OF WORKING IN DEVELOPMENT EDUCATION

There are twenty assignments listed above. One can get an idea of the technical challenges related to each from the project and work description. One may also imagine the working environment. Each culture and working environment will be quite different. To help you think about the human side of development work, a little story about a project Chief of Party and his local Counterpart follows. There are as many cultures as national projects and there are as many kinds of Chiefs of Party and local Counterparts. One might say that cultures have a personality. And certainly cultures are inhabited by people of distinctive personality. We succeed in development work by the relationships that we build, just as much as we do by the quality of our professional work. The exchange that follows speaks to the importance of relationships in development and suggests the mystery that accompanies cross cultural endeavors. The mystery incidentally, is a two way affair. It is not something to be inhibited by, rather it is something to be intrigued and challenged by, something interesting – even fascinating.

Relevant Story

He was a small man with a big smile. Very articulate but quiet. Mr. Pitso had had a long career in education. Among other things over the years, he worked as a teacher and school principal, as head of a teacher's college, and as a curriculum developer. He had a nice family. Mrs. Pitso was very gracious, modest, and organized. There were two young adult sons. They were polite and obviously well raised. Mr. Pitso was a writer. He was extremely interested in language and was compiling reference books and a dictionary. He was concerned about orthography – that his native language was too often improperly spoken or written, that because it was used throughout southern Africa by millions of people of very different situations, standard proper usage was being lost. He was respected at Ministry institutions (the Curriculum Centre, Teacher's College, Materials Development Centre, Teacher Service Commission, University, Distance Teaching Centre, Inspectorate, and the Exams Council). He was also well known by the nation's schools as someone academically oriented rather than politically motivated. He was not interested in power or prestige but rather concerned about education. Mr. Pitso got on with Ministry leadership but was also respected by leaders from the Catholic, Anglican, Methodist, Adventist, and Reformed schools.

When the project needed someone from the Ministry full time, someone to work as the Chief of Party's counterpart, the Ministry sought out Thabo Pitso. Although busy with academic projects, he agreed. The potential of the project to improve the national school system excited him. And so it was that the project Chief of Party (COP) was working closely with Mr. Pitso.

In fact, at 10 on this Saturday morning the COP would be going over to Thabo's house. There were things to discuss.

Eight A.M. on a Saturday and the project Chief of Party was at the office. It was one of those fresh African mornings. The roosters of the city had gone silent a few hours ago. The skies were absolutely clear, lots of birds in the trees, flowers in full bloom: roses, bottle bush trees, red poker, and virtually no traffic on Constitution Avenue. A few cows grazed along the streets. As he looked out the office window the COP wondered what might be going on at home. Let's see, the U.S. was about 12,000 miles in that – no that direction. He looked in the direction of Johannesburg, some five driving hours away over the high veld. Then he looked just a little to the left. Yes, some fourteen hours by air in that direction, that would be where New York is, he thought.

Without willing it, he began to think of things people might be doing this morning. What a wonderful diverse world. Someone was feverishly driving a taxi in Manhattan, another, an Amish person, was driving a horse drawn wagon in New York's Seneca County. A man was hitting a golf ball in Chapel Hill. A Florida woman was slipping into a swimming pool. In Bangladesh someone was leading a Water Buffalo. Another person was beating cotton on a rooftop. Up country here, women were carrying water buckets on their heads – perfect posture. His brother could well be in the air between New York and Rio. His eldest son in New York would be going to bed. His son in Nevada would already be sleeping. His daughter in Rome was on the same time as here.

Amazing how busily different we are this morning, he thought. His imagination took him to places he had worked or visited. There would be people on the Star Ferry between Kowloon and Hong Kong, others in a cable car on Capetown's Table Mountain, a man driving an eighteen wheeler in Central Germany, and two men poling a dugout through the Okavango Delta in Botswana. People selling fish on Sri Lankan beaches and an Eskimo studying ice flows in the Mackenzie. A dazzling Hindu bride receiving gifts, a boy and girl playing Frisbee with their Golden Retriever on majestic Cape Breton, monks in meditation at a beautiful temple in Thailand's Chaing Mai, the colorful changing of the Guard in Ottawa, people climbing steps to enter the 1000 rooms that are Tibet's historic, mysterious, and holy Potala Palace, and a band in ancient Durbar Square of Kathmandu. The pictures exhilarated him. What a fascinating world.

The Chief of Party drove his elderly but trusty Peugeot along Constitution Avenue, turning onto Caledon Road just before the Prime Minister's residence. He remembered being told that his teenage son and a friend used to taunt the guards there. A bad idea he thought. Caledon went down a large hill. You could look directly into another country from here. Shadowy blue mountains dotted the far away landscape. Right onto Industrial Road and then past the recruiting offices for coal, diamond, and gold miners and into a narrow lane leading to new brick houses huddled against a hill. He walked through an old fashioned gate. The house, like most here, was walled off from the road. Vines with blue flowers crept over the brick. Mr. Pitso saw him coming and threw open the door. "Come in, come in, you're just in time for morning tea." An attractive brick house, well cared for grounds, and fine furniture locally made.

"So tell me Mr. Pitso, are we being too sophisticated with the project? Are we going too far beyond basic needs? Are we attempting to do too much at once?" Mr. Pitso reflected for a few moments. It was his habit to let silence intervene. He also sort of wrapped one arm behind his neck so that his left hand touched his right ear when in deep contemplation. "The way I see it, is that this is a once in a lifetime opportunity for education here. The project is the project. Yes it is a huge. Yes it is far reaching and complicated. It is indeed an easy target for some

people – for those who feel the Ministry has given over too many decisions, for those who feel project planning was not participatory enough, those who look for political motivation behind all development assistance, those who feel intruded upon, for those who do not want change, those who don't want to work and who are embarrassed by people who do." They both laughed. The COP interjected, "How are we going to make progress if so many suspect us?" And then he went on, "Every part of this project makes sense, every part is needed, every part has fine local people connected with it. But I can certainly appreciate that some don't understand it and are suspicious." Mr. Pitso added, "You know of course, that perhaps the biggest challenge we face is the fact that we have to somehow understand and match, in the best that way we can, two very different cultures that do business in two very different ways".

"It will come down to the relationship that each Advisor establishes," Mr. Pitso went on. "You personally have the trust of people throughout the Ministry. But your people will have to establish it for themselves. Another thing to keep in mind – those who oppose will pretty much just not participate. The others and I think they are in the majority, will move ahead."

The Chief of Party leaned forward. "You know Thabo, I personally think the project is too big, too involved, too ambitious, and too bureaucratic for a short five years. Frankly it's a lot for a country like this to deal with. But I agree with you. It offers tremendous resources and wonderful opportunities. We have no choice but to work at it in sincerity, to make it as genuinely participatory as we can, and to just explain over and over, hoping that people will understand. I think we need to be as open as possible – need to let people recreate parts of the project so as to better address needs, accommodate local processes, and proceed at a realistic pace. I realize of course, that the thinking of each government on project objectives, contractual obligations, and the momentum of foreign management limits us in terms of refashioning efforts.

But the major players want the best out of this thing for the sake of the kids here. If we can just get to them – just explain well enough, I'm sure people will agree to appropriate changes at the right times."

Mr. Pitso stroked his hair. "I appreciate your taking such a view. I'll work with you to the fullest to see that it all comes together. Know though, that I've come to understand, at least a little, how very complex things are for you with respect to contracts and subcontracts, the specificity of outcomes, the tied release of monies, and so on. I admire your willingness to be flexible and to have things recreated as we go along, but I know what you are up against. Anyway, let us give it our all."

Both had been at the project long enough to know about the orientation and workings of major project players, i.e. The Cabinet, the Ministry of Education, the local Development Assistance Mission, offices in Washington, the prime contractor, and the seven organizations who held subcontracts.

For obvious reasons, Mr. Pitso was more in the know about local things than the COP. This was really the reason for a Saturday morning meeting. Mrs. Pitso brought more tea. Thabo began, "First of all we both know that the project design is excellent, a work of genius. It is comprehensive, systematic, has good and direct linkages between inputs and outcomes. The project paper writers had a real handle on our system, on the functions and interrelationship of things like philosophy, curriculum, materials, training, and what eventually happens in the nation's classrooms. And certainly those who responded to the RFP and wrote the winning proposal were outstanding. The plan for pulling it all off is excellent. But, I agree with you. It's kind of too much too soon. Perhaps we should be allowed to piece it together over ten years rather than five." The COP reacted quickly. "Thabo, the designers have inputs and outcomes right. But the process between is laced with intrigue in a cross-cultural situation of such profound differences. We're talking cultural confrontation in a way. I mean how things happen here does not square with how things happen in the West. Maybe twenty years would be more realistic than ten. The process – takes time! All of the technique and technology in the world won't do it. All of the professional advice, all the resources are good and necessary, given the goals. But, the political and cultural process – a design can't really speak to that. We've got to figure it out as we go along – got to work outside and beyond. In the West, I suppose that x and y inputs and actions are predictable in terms of outcome. Not here, Thabo." Mr. Pitso laughed.

Mr. Pitso related some of the things going on, on the local scene that the Chief of Party should know about – things that might be affecting the work of their team. One of Mr. Pitso's sons came by. "More tea, some biscuits?" Taking a biscuit the COP said, "Kealebua."

"I spoke with the Director of NCDC on Friday afternoon. It seems that he and his staff are getting along well with the advisors. I haven't heard complaints about any of them." Thabo was speaking about the National Curriculum Centre where the project was helping with new curricula, test instruments, learning materials, radio instruction, outreach and dissemination, and teacher development in the field.

The Chief of Party asked what local managers were saying to Mr. Pitso at other places where the project was working. "Well, the head of NTTC seems to be pleased with each of them." Project advisors were working hand in hand with staff at the Teachers College on curricula, teaching methods, agricultural education, financial management, general operations management, and academic planning.

The Chief of Party gave a little sigh of relief. "Good news Thabo. You never know. These folks get into some pretty sensitive areas

– get into other people's business. That's their work. What about IMRC? Hear anything this week about our staff over there?"

"I haven't been able to sit down with the director. So far as I know, the first advisors are still considered indispensable."

Thabo was speaking of the old guard at the Resource Development Centre. The COP jumped in, "What about the others?"

"Yes, right, I haven't heard anything bad – I assume they are still doing well."

At the IMRC (the Instructional Materials Centre), project personnel were working with local staff on materials design, printing, radio productions, video presentations, exam production, library development, computer instruction, and the like. A busy place. "Pretty practical stuff Thabo, things that people can immediately see as beneficial."

Mrs. Pitso appeared. The Chief of Party guessed that perhaps it was time for him to move along – people did their shopping on Saturday mornings. Grocery and dry goods stores would close at noon. "Well Thabo, I think I had better get home to see if my wife needs me to go to the O.K. Bazaar or anyplace."

"Alright, let us talk about the School Supply Unit and Teacher Service Commission another time."

"Don't forget the Training Centre at Thaba Tseka, Thabo. I'd like to know what your people are saying about our work up there. It's a big challenge." Mr. Pitso thought for a minute. "Well, we should discuss some other things next week as well – the Evening College, Adult Literacy, and the District Resource Teacher Project. What am I forgetting?" The Chief of Party noted the work on job descriptions and personnel policies in which project advisors were involved.

Thabo added, "And next time we should also talk about the vast amount of training that is going on and whether placements are good." The COP thought about an unfortunate incident in which a local person had been involved overseas but decided to leave it alone.

Before leaving the Chief of Party said, almost to himself, "You know, I don't understand really. It seems like virtually every local counterpart and every local boss is happy with the advisors assigned to them. It seems like people recognize how very hard all of the project people are working. And you have to admit – the output is phenomenal. And yet, I sense a general unease. It's like (this is great – we are really producing together but I'll be glad when it's over and we can get back to how things were before.) Whenever I talk with key individuals on the Ministry side, I get some pretty positive vibes. On a one to one basis, things seem to be going well. But on a more general basis, there seems to be this low fevered disquiet, this discomfort, this sense of intrusion somehow. Am I being too harsh Thabo or is my sense right?"

Mr. Pitso didn't blink an eye. "I don't think the excellent work of individuals is questioned. And I think most of my people would agree that valuable things are being done for education in this country. It's something deeper. I don't understand it myself. However, remember we are right in the middle of a cross-cultural and nettlesome thicket. Pretty interesting. I wouldn't worry about it." The Chief of Party got up to leave. "Promise me that we can pick up on this conversation early next week Thabo. OK? Good," Mr.Pitso replied with a gentle smile.

Chapter VII
Working in Volunteer Development Organizations

T here are many development organizations that work through dedicated volunteers. Often, such organizations have considerable permanent staff as well. The Peace Corps for example, depending on the country in which it is operating and depending on the composition of its programs, has expatriate staff who are there for a few years and long term local employees. Together they handle responsibilities in the areas of representation/administration, recruitment, finance, transportation, housing, medical care, professional supplies, host country relations, training, programming, evaluation, and reporting. However, most of the personnel in a Peace Corps Mission are carefully selected and well trained volunteers who carry out the development work to which the organization is obligated throughout the host country.

Like the American Peace Corps, there are many organizations which are national or international volunteer agencies, e.g. Australian Volunteers, Canada Corps, Canadian University Service Overseas, Japan International Cooperation Agency (JICA), World Friends Korea, FK Norway, United Nations Volunteers, Voluntary Service Overseas, European Volunteer Service, and Sri Lanka

Volunteers. However, there are many volunteer centered organizations working in development or relief which are not part of a national government or international agency. A few examples may be readily familiar: Habitat for Humanity, International Red Cross, Red Crescent Movement, CCIVS, Concordia Youth Service Volunteers, Hermitage Volunteer Service, Hope Development Volunteers, Young Adult Volunteer Program, Operation Crossroads Africa, Worldwide Helpers, One Heart Source, Medecins Sans Frontiers, United Way Worldwide, A Better World, Peace Brigades International, Humanity World International, Service Civil International, Service Nation, TECHO, Society of Saint Vincent de Paul, Building a Better Future, Volunteers in Asia, and Volunteer Service Abroad.

Different Approaches by Different Organizations

Some organizations which work through volunteers provide for lengthy assignments. For example, the standard Peace Corps assignment is 27 months. Some Peace Corps volunteers extend for a second tour. Peace Corp volunteers have primary assignments and most also develop a second initiative that they work at when not busy with their primary assignment. A primary assignment might be for example, high school teaching, nursing in a remote clinic, providing instruction on the avoidance of serious decease, or helping a community cope with living in an HIV or Malaria environment. A volunteer's secondary initiative might be for example, community organizing and fund raising that will ultimately result in a school or community library. Hence, because a volunteer is in a community for a year or two, there may be considerable potential for project work. This though would be different than the project work described earlier in the book, where teams of advisors work with counterparts, some times for four or five years on involved national institution building. The Peace Corps does work to organize efforts into integrated programs and no doubt this contributes to greater community impact.

Organizations that work through volunteers who have more or less short term tours in host countries, may take a different approach. For example, some might assign volunteers for a relatively short to medium period to observe an election, give lectures on micro finance, hold an eye surgery clinic, collect air quality data, observe refugee living conditions, convene a political negotiation, measure conditions related to climate change, gather information that would be used later in the design of a dam, give lectures on safe water, or advocate for homeless children.

In either case, work through volunteers across the developing world is fascinating, creative, and greatly needed. I recall for example, a volunteer teacher in the remote high mountains of Central Asia who on the side, developed a hydroelectric capacity from fast flowing mountain waters and provided electricity to communities, which from the beginning of time, had been completely dark at sundown. One could go on to list hundreds of incredible projects.

FOCUSING ON ONE VOLUNTEER ORGANIZATION

In order to focus this chapter, let us concentrate on the Peace Corps. We could as well analyze the work of another volunteer-oriented organization and find it just as fascinating. Let me start by telling a story.

One by one they straggled out*. Their plane had arrived at Moshoeshoe International Airport just minutes ago. Not all fifty four of them were there yet. Some were on another airplane not far behind. They would join 90 volunteers already in the country. Clearing immigration and customs was easy, the way smoothed ahead of time by local staff of the Peace Corps Mission in the country. Coming into the main lobby, they were wide-eyed. Twenty one hours after leaving New York and traveling via*

Europe, they were finally stepping onto African soil. As they came through the door, they were shell shocked, jet lagged, and sobered as local people and a few American staff members reached to shake their hands. "Welcome, welcome Meagan, we are glad you are here." "Welcome Evan, very glad you are joining us." One by one they met the Peace Corps Country Director, the Associate Director for Education, the Chief Medical Officer, the Associate Director for Administration, the Director of Training, several other staff members, and a handful of Volunteers who had been here for many months.

Other staff members and local hosts were waiting for them at Our Lady's House some twenty miles away over a road that circled breathtaking mountain peaks, site of the twelve week pre-service training these volunteers would begin next week. After collecting bags they passed into the airport parking lot. The day was very bright but the temperature was comfortable with a cloudless sky and clear and clean air. No town in sight. Wide open space. Across an erosion scared valley, blue mountains, some that seemed to be wearing a round hat, dominated the landscape. Layer upon layer of them for as far as one could see. In the field immediately beyond the parking lot, three plows were pulled by muscle bound oxen. Women walked distant paths, baskets balanced on their heads.

The ride to Roma and Our Lady's House was eventful; it had steep roads with sharp unguarded curves. The occasional Leyland bus belched black smoke from coal based liquid fuel. Each carried bags, kids, and small livestock on the roof. Men in colorful and flowing blankets on horseback seemed confident of their right of way. Clothes spread out to dry on boulders along the banks of mountain streams. Women worked the fabrics back and forth, back and forth, in crystal clear waters. Children bathed in their birthday suits. At the end of a straight away was a small store with a horse drawn wagon in front. A road sign read Thaba Bosiu. After a time, they would learn of its historic and almost sacred significance. On one side stood a brown stone building. They would come to learn of the significance to the country of mission schools. And coming around a sharp bend, there, way down there, they could see the Roma Valley which they had been told about at orientation in Washington. The Combi (minivan) descended slowly. Unlike the countryside so far, the Roma Valley was heavy with large Evergreen and Eucalyptus trees. In side valleys, one could see many clusters of stone buildings – private secondary schools and seminaries. The National University in the distance stood in a meadow of its own.

As one young woman peered out her window, she thought about a book she had read on Africa of times past. She wondered if any of that remained. Were roles anywhere near as differentiated as in that book? Was the property still owned by men? Were there cases remaining of multiple wives – each with a distinct role? Is it still so that in prominent families, a girl might inherit even her father's social position and be given the male title? Do women still do a great deal of the field work, their children gathered around to help, and is this an impediment to school attendance? If a woman needs surgery or other serious medical care, is she dependent on her husband, or his brothers for permission, if he is away? What are the trends now concerning fidelity and community cohesiveness? She would observe carefully she thought. She was convinced that Peace Corps volunteers should learn as much about the culture as possible, as quickly as possible, otherwise one might do more harm than good. Actually, those were her father's words. She did not agree with some of the volunteers she had gotten to know. One young man thought the job of a volunteer is to bring western values and ways of doing things to these people. So far though, she had kept this to herself. She wondered how many of the new volunteers might see it her way. Still, she did not think she had it all figured out and maybe those who would disagree with her were more in the know than she.

The Combi slowed. To the left she could read a sign saying Christ the King High School. To the right she read a sign that said St. Joseph's Hospital.

And then they entered a narrow rutted trail with tall trees on both sides, as if planted carefully a hundred years ago. At the end of this road they came upon Our Lady's House. The Combi shifted down, crept over exposed tree roots and came to a stop under giant Eucalyptus trees. There were women in front of the vehicle singing joyously. They were dressed in colorful blankets. This was obviously a song of welcome. Several shoeless boys stood to one side shyly.

As they disembarked, everyone in the world came to shake their hands. After regrouping, Me' Mothe, Director of Training, went over the day's schedule with them. Assistant Director of Training, Lephoto, showed them to their rooms. Neat and clean but rustic. For the most part, those riding in the Combi were Florina's. Florina Pheko was Associate Peace Corps Director for Education. The young lady who had thoughtfully gazed out the window along the way could not take her eyes off Me' Florina. She was striking. Florina had seen several classes come and then sadly go after two years.

She stood next to the Peace Corps Country Director. "What do you think of them Ntate Don?" He looked at her for a moment. Both of them knew first impressions could be misleading in this business. The unpredictability of living and working day after day in a very different culture seemed to strengthen most but eroded a few. Sometimes those who seemed most confident at first arrival had a set back after coming face to face with the complexities of living and working in a new world. Trying to work in a system so different from your own was a challenge some found exhilarating but that a few seemed to find disturbing. Sometimes those who at first were meek, tentative, and hesitant grew day by day, until they were obviously comfortable in the

role of partner but also of leader. "They seem like a fine group"
he said.

Me' Florina and Don were impressed with this new group. As far
as they could tell after such limited contact, the new volunteers
were personable without exception. So far, even after a grueling
trip and now faced with the inconveniences of life in a
developing country, the new volunteers were not complaining.
Certainly they all came highly recommended. The Peace Corps
was as careful as possible in the recruitment process and in
making selections. Selections had to be in keeping with the
design of country programs and the needs of assignments, as
seen by Peace Corps staff in the field and as seen by local
partners. Specifications on each position being recruited for were
always thoughtfully worked up by Peace Corps field staff in
concert with the local people who would work with and supervise
them, as well as by officials of the Ministry under which the work
would be done. Then Peace Corps Washington searched and
interviewed carefully to get the right match between demand
and supply. This could take several months. They would have a
good preliminary orientation stateside. Me' Florina and the
Country Director knew that technical expertise would be no
problem. If anyone were to have a problem after a time, it would
have to do with working relationships, disagreement on
approaches to the work, culturally based frustrations, and
psychological coping.

On the whole though, the volunteers would make out just fine,
partly because the organization was well organized and
managed. The Peace Corps staff in this beautiful mountain
country was especially proud of the program that had been
worked up over many years. One hundred and forty volunteers
worked in many exciting and productive initiatives – primary
school teaching, secondary school teaching, small business
development, water development (extremely important in a
parched land), environmental conservation, fisheries

development, healthcare, public institution management, community based agricultural, school self-reliance, and range management. In addition, the Peace Corps operated a million dollar agricultural development project on contract to the local USAID and the host government. It also had recently taken on an effort that would be partially funded by USAID, and which would result in the construction of 88 community water systems. The Peace Corps here worked closely with other volunteer organizations: the Canadians, British, Irish, Germans, Danish, and with area NGO's and various government Ministries.

COMING FACE TO FACE WITH THEIR ASSIGNMENT

"What's on after they get settled Florina?"

"They have free time until after dinner and then in early evening, we will review the first week's schedule with them. The Director reflected on the great training the volunteers would have over the next three months and then the periodic shorter trainings for special purposes. They would become speakers of a foreign language – able to actually work in it. They would get in-depth instruction about another culture, another part of the world with a special history. They would come face to face with other values but learn that fundamentally humankind is more alike than not. And most fascinating to many of them would be the age old simmering conflict of the region, based on socio-economic matters completely new to them and grounded in what different groups of the region honestly thought was a struggle for survival. They would be oriented to a different system of governance and learn the ins and outs of power here. Much of this would be learned in Peace Corps trainings but most would be absorbed just by being here. The partnerships and social interactions they would have with other development organizations from around the world would be fascinating and a great education. The best way, he thought, to learn about *worldwide development initiatives is from the field. They would leave here many months from now with a great education. And they would have developed contacts with organizations that could ultimately prove valuable in terms of a career in development.*

"And tomorrow?" he asked Florina.

"They have been encouraged to take a walk before breakfast. After breakfast Dr. Sara and the nurses will begin health briefings and procedures. And a little later in the morning Bill and Margaret will do briefings on some administrative matters – interim allowances, lost baggage, transportation, and so on. Wayne and Nancy will do a session on host country – Peace Corps relationships and protocols at 10:00. We plan to emphasize the central role of the Peace Corps Program Officers. That needs to be clear from the start. And then Ntate, if you could bring the Ambassador in at 11 for the official welcome, that would be great. Will you and he be able to stay for lunch?"

"Of course, we would not miss it," he said.

"Then at two we thought we would have your session on Peace Corps philosophy, our expectations of the volunteers, and introducing them to vital information about the people of this country. That should set the stage for important questions and then for informal discussions amount themselves in the days ahead."

Florina was called away. Don remained on the veranda. I wonder, he thought, I wonder why each of them has come. Adventure? To test themselves? Travel? Political commitment at this turning point in the region? To give back in gratitude for something? He figured that most of them probably had a mixture of motives. He guessed that compassion played a role for some of them in some way, and that service was important.

And he wondered if any of them were trying to get away from something at home. His attitude was that there is no right or wrong reason, so long as each is conscientious about their work and is respectful toward their hosts.

A Peugot Bakkie (pickup) drove up without his notice. "Are you going down to the city tonight?" It was Patrick Bereng. They had known each other for a long time. Patrick taught at the university, was editor of the university newspaper, and a poet. He was also a descendant of the great King Moshoeshoe, savior of his people. They sat quietly for a bit, taking in the great expanses, the high peaks, and ponies on the high plateaus, free to do as they wished. Don invited Patrick to stay for lunch and he said yes. The Ambassador's car drove in. As a Chief of Party in various parts of the world, and now as Country Director of the Peace Corps, Don had known several Ambassadors. This one was his favorite. They were good friends.

INTRODUCTORY DISCUSSION ON THEIR WORK

The Ambassador left just before Don's afternoon session. The new volunteers joined him in front of Our Lady's House. This was the kick off to what would be a three day orientation on service and the host country. That would be integrated with four additional days of orientation on policies, administration, health, security, job placement, transportation, and related issues. Some of the local people with whom volunteers will work would be present.

His greeting to the new volunteers was "Khotso Bo Me and Le Bo Ntate. (Peace to you ladies and gentlemen). We are honored you have come to live and work with us. Beside our families, you are the most important people in our lives now. Because we won't be all together often, allow me to share some serious thoughts this afternoon.

My experiences in this country have been very special. Indeed it's a special place, a precious place, precious for its remote stillness and the clearest skies on earth. It's special for its soul enriching warmth and the civility of its people, for the cooing of mourning doves, the security people have in family, and for unselfish sharing. You will find it is special for the tinkling of distant cow bells and the hushed breezes through Mimosa trees. This country is special because of the respect given to its elders and for the time people have for each other. It's special because of the refreshing lack of pretension among people who are ever ready to smile and help. In these hills, there is innocence while much of the world has entered an age of cynical self-promotion. There are friends to be had and friendships that will last forever. As you get to know this part of the world, as you experience its hard way of life and come to understand its history, you will marvel at a people who have hope where there has seemingly been little reason for hope. You will become incredulous that there is love where there should be antagonism. You will see that there can be patience where there should be frustration and trust where there should be discontent. Let this place teach you! Let us take lessons from this place for our work together.

But as special as this place is, there will be some tough times ahead, you know. When those come along we can become frustrated and drive each other mad or we can work things out with civility. We can resolve right now to ever be supportive of each other. And we can resolve to always extend civility and support beyond ourselves to our hosts. In fact, that is one thing I will always insist on, respect for our hosts.

You know, you are about to become involved in some of the most fundamental issues of our age. Watch for them, think hard about them. You are going to have opportunities that few Americans ever have – opportunities to be of service to another people and in so doing, become better people yourselves. You are going to have the time out here to truly get to know people. You will be able to learn from each other. You will be able to share life in every sense. Your years here will let you see the good in a people who are very different from you. In your heart you will become one with them, taking their challenges as your own and feeling what they feel. You can if you allow it, become enriched by people of a history and culture new to you. If you are like most who have gone before you, you will come to cherish what another people have become." He asked that they put aside notions they might have developed about the country from books and conversations, and be prepared to see things from a fresh perspective. "The background you have from books and such will be helpful but what you will learn now, from first-hand experience, will overshadow it significantly if you are truly open to it." He also asked them to keep in mind that every so called developing country is very different. None of them are likely to fit the model you have built up in your mind. The range of economic development among developing countries is vast. So too is the range of everything else.

I sincerely hope you will take the next few weeks to observe carefully, to reflect on what you see, to ponder and to wonder. What is this place all about? Why?" He noted that after the orientations they would get here, and at Peace Corps headquarters in the next few days, they would have an opportunity to observe and begin to assemble ideas on what this place was all about, because they would be doing a one week village live–in, someplace in the country. That would be followed by time together again, here at Our Lady's House, where they would debrief, discuss their experiences, and ask more questions. He said their Program Officers would discuss the complete timetable of in-service training sessions they would have over the next two years, before this first seven days of orientation finished. The Country Director went on to discuss topics like inherited place and protocol, the sense of time in rural parts of the country, family life, and village cohesiveness.

Don suddenly stopped and invited questions and comments. Being in the place discussed, and being on the edge of an assignment that would immerse each of them in another life, the new volunteers asked questions with excitement. He had always thought that teaching in close proximity to where and when one has to apply that teaching, is a key to learning, no matter the topic, because one is so motivated by the situation. In answer to various questions, he told his audience to start by just getting to know people, be more interested in them than in telling them about yourself. His responses to volunteer questions left bits of advice like this. "Try to figure out what is really valued here." "Try not to take over conversations – be the one learning at first, and be seen as here to be of service on the matters which are of importance to them." "Show that you truly want to know about your hosts and their challenges, so that you can be of help in your new community. You will build trust, credibility and personal legitimacy in this way." "Without the trust, credibility and legitimacy, that only your hosts can confer, you will be dead in the water." "For a time, be stingy with your observations. It is easy to be pretty far out on observations in a place you know so little of. Give it time. People will see through shallowness. Also, these modest and humble people are not likely to be very forthcoming if you just take over." "You will have lots of time to share your expertise and even give some advice after you are well established, after you truly understand the context, and after you have become accepted as one with them." "While it is probably not necessary to say, let me suggest you refrain from criticizing their ways of doing things, the way they prioritize, and so forth. There will be other ways of working after you know more." "There is a history to everything here that you do not know yet, there are long standing social reasons for how things are done which you do not understand yet, there is a relationship with the environment that you do not sense yet." "Be willing to get into your work step by step, and to go along with things that don't seem to be related to the task at hand." "Remember this has been a very agrarian country for centuries. It is a place of seasonal routines. Events are cyclical. It is not a place of beginning and ending orientation, as we know it. Social process and ritual is very important, perhaps more so than result or product." "In large measure this is not a change oriented place. In fact, in some cases change can be seen as threatening to order and lifestyle."

This set off a lot of discussion and led volunteers to analyze their own homeland. The questions kept coming and answers were given. "Ritual is sort of like insulation on a wire. It protects from overheating, from shorting and from flame out. There is no shortage of ritual here. But let me warn you. You are so used to straight forward efficiency and unadorned productivity that this place will at first drive you mad. You will know that things like being together, doing things together and so on, are more important than productivity here, but even though you understand that, you will find it almost impossible to deal with, at least in the early days. For me, a balance would be good but that balance does not exist, either out here or back at home. You are going to have to deal with that in some fashion, once you have moved to your village."

A volunteer who had been in the country for a year stood up and began to quietly distribute a short handout. It read:

The Peace Corps, what a great organization! Founded in 1961 by President John F. Kennedy who challenged the citizens of his time, "Ask not what your country can do for you but what you can do for your country." Since then, the Peace Corps has sent 210,000 volunteers into the world, each for two years of service, some for twice that. One hundred and thirty nine countries have been served by the Peace Corps. Currently with 8,073 volunteers at work, the Peace Corps represents every American group and is in North, East, West, and Southern Africa, Latin America, Eastern Europe, Central, East, and South Asia, the

Caribbean, the Middle East, and the Pacific Islands. It has been referred to as the greatest graduate school going. Surely it is a great investment. How can you beat an annual budget of 375 million dollars when the United States has government agencies that have annual budgets in the billions? An organization that does so much on less than the water or snow removal monies spent by major cities.

Me' Mothe got to her feet. "Any more questions for the Director?" she asked. A hand went up.

"You mentioned that achieving things will not be as straightforward as it would be for us at home. Could you explain that a little more?"

Don thought for a minute before answering. "Incidentally, we have quite a few of our host country staff here this afternoon and I would invite them to chip in any time they wish." He looked at the three trainers who sat to one side of the volunteer audience. "Well perhaps I should have said that for us, things will often not get done as we think they should. For us sometimes, things will not seem straightforward. But for the local people, they will not seem unusual at all. I'm sure some of the things we might wonder about are perfectly understandable to the citizens of this country. The country is still quite cohesive. For good historic reasons, protecting one's own is a virtue. Embarrassing one's own is shameful. When this is transported out of the villages to more urban settings, it can seem like Nepotism. But in actual fact it is not. In the extended family and in the ancient villages, people were obligated to look after their own. And now when many are in larger towns and small cities, work and family life are not yet separated. So, management has to straddle two worlds, just as you will need to do. We could spend a lot of time examining how things work differently here. You will have plenty of time for that in the months ahead. My point is this. In order to operate successfully, you will have to learn how things happen.

That's a good way of putting it, because sometimes you will notice that something just happened and you will ask yourself, 'Now how did that happen?'" This brought laughter. "What makes the community or institution with which you are working tick? You will need to understand. After all, your goal should be to build it up. When you have a better understanding and have established credibility, you will judiciously begin to help with some changes. But your big challenge at first will be to figure out how things are done."

He thought about the advice he had just given and decided to balance it a bit. "I don't mean to make this sound like a big problem. It is not. Believe me, you will find that people take you in with open arms – so long as you are not arrogant and have what they perceive as a partnership attitude. You will be amazed at the warmth of these people, their interest in you, and their willingness to work with you. Don't be surprised if some of them become a bit protective of you. But they will be sensitive to your attitude toward them. After all, it can be awkward for respected members of a community to receive help. We can make it difficult to operate here if someone leaves the impression that they look down on their hosts." A period of silence took over. Then one of the trainers spoke up and asked for a little more explanation on the straddling of two worlds. Don spoke as if thinking about every word. "Well, the modern sector is a relatively new layer in this society. In the west you can know one's responsibilities and authority by reading their job description. Here, managers in the modern sector have job descriptions too. But there is an older and higher authority throughout this place. Perhaps most of the time, there is no problem and a manager moves along ok. And sometimes that does not happen. You will need to watch and listen so that you can learn. Relationships are more important than the system and can sometimes have a significant impact."

He reflected again for a moment and then added a point that he had not planned on. "You know, I am very glad you are starting your career with the Peace Corps. It is a great organization that will allow you to work at a realistic level of development. In my opinion, it is a big advantage for someone in this work to start their career in the field, dealing with a nation's and a people's real and most urgent problems. Later in your career you may find yourself in some sort of senior position in a development bureaucracy. Those positions can be fascinating and one can do a lot of good in them. But if one does not have a solid down to earth grounding in the field, they can on occasion, unwittingly do harm. To an extent, we have that sort of problem anywhere, including at home. But it can be more complicated in a cross-cultural situation. Sometimes those who design development projects or programs get carried away with the latest thing in their professional field and it does not fit. Often too, senior planners are influenced more than they know, by the latest systems for managing and measuring large operations. Applying them to a particular project design might just not be congruent with where a host people are or want to go. And it can drive implementers crazy.

You know, as a development specialist, it is more important that you are tuned into the horizontal than the vertical, that is, that you know the people around you, that you know their real needs and that you know how to get things accomplished with them. But our professions, our bureaucracies, and perhaps our very culture insists we give a lot of attention to the vertical, that is to say, that we follow the script set out for us by our professional discipline, the bureaucracy behind us, the contract that has been given to us and the specific design someone far away has created for the projects we work on. It is not realistic to ignore the vertical but we must not lose sight of the horizontal in the process, because if we achieve great things that are given to be achieved by the vertical, and they are not important to those all around us, the horizontal will all be meaningless. I'll stop here.

We can talk about these things sometime if you wish." He knew this topic would be brought up again soon by the most thoughtful volunteers. Being in the field for a short time would induce it. His experience had always been that Peace Corps volunteers are pretty inquisitive and analytical.

The sound of bells – a shepherd and small herd passing by. A late afternoon chill in the air. Smoke from distant fires was beginning to curl skyward. The smell of wood became obvious. Uniformed school girls finished for the day, walked across the nearby field singing. Water was being carried into Our Lady's House kitchen. A late afternoon chapel bell rang quietly. Two pony riders were silhouetted on the ridge nearest to them.

The group continued the discussion. In answer to questions, Don and other staff members offered information like, "Peers often keep each other in line here for the sake of social stability." "Individualism gone too far is frowned upon." "Those in a family who have, are supposed to give whatever is needed to less fortunate family members." A trainer noted that his country has an incredible respect for inherited position and for convention. He said that in light of this, "Consensus decision making is not a convenience, it is a virtue." In response, some of the volunteers began a side discussion on the importance of somehow sinking deep roots here. They very quietly talked together about the responsibilities they would likely have and made guesses about how it would be different from the same tasks at home.

Another trainer spoke up. He introduced himself as Ntate Moshebesha. A handsome man with a wonderful smile. "Perhaps one of the most important things you should learn before going out to your sites is, "What are the most inappropriate behaviors in a remote village." This caused worried looks. Sensing the concern, Me' Florina interjected, "Not to worry volunteers, we will have a session on that before you leave here. It is not complicated, just common sense."

A middle aged woman introduced herself as Marion, a volunteer who has already been in the country for a year and a half. She spoke about how one comes to love peaceful mountain living with its wonderful vistas, clear air, beautiful sunrises, country sounds that carry great distances, children who sing for you without prompting, people who never fail to greet you with courtesy, the respect everyone shows you and the simple gifts children bring you, sometimes from their parents, sometimes from themselves. She mentioned how she has grown fond of her mountain riding pony. She said she is grateful that there are so many little things she can do that help people, like answering a question about the world climate, setting someone up with a business records book, helping a child read a story, and telling someone the reason for a practice that promotes good hygiene. Then she spoke briefly about traditions. "There are reasons for everything; it is just that we don't always know them. Some of them you can sort of surmise by piecing things together. For example, I would guess that people in places like this around the world have developed a long standing psychological mechanism for dealing with disasters. I would call it stoic acceptance of what comes. When you think of how vulnerable these people have been over the centuries, it makes sense as a survival strategy. If you do not already know, you will learn of things like the incredible great Mfecane (famine that extended over an entire land), historic droughts, Zulu attacks, Boer invasions, and so on and you will see why some sort of survival psychology became necessary." She went on to talk about the fact that the country people are not materialistic and not very acquisitive and she challenged the new volunteers to reflect on this for a reason. She told them they will probably struggle to figure what motivates people. "You know, Maslow breaks down in the rural areas and most of the country is rural. And we have thought it is a universal law," she smiled.

Another volunteer who has been in the country for nearly two years decided to speak. He was passing through on the way to

Peace Corps headquarters. His work site was "about two days in that direction", he pointed. Introducing himself as Jeff, he noted that Marion's thoughts had triggered some of his own that might be helpful. He said he thought it important to know that this is not a compulsive culture. "People here are probably more committed to being than doing, although my Peace Corps friends who are posted in the capital city inform me this is changing significantly." Living in a remote area, he had had time to give this a lot of thought. "The master that was apparently internalized during the industrial revolution was not internalized here," he stated. "At least that is a theory I have developed. So people here are still quite outer directed; directed by social convention. This has helped me understand things when I have expected something to happen that does not materialize."

His remarks caused a bit of a stir. After a few moments, Me'Mothe stepped forward again, "Ok it is nearly time for dinner. I am going to ask Nate Don to make the final remark before we eat."

"Alright, in closing for the day let me leave you with this thought. This country, like any other, has a unique history. Its people have had unique experiences. Over the centuries they have developed their own way of dealing with things. Even the sensory environment is unique. Now, of course, people value what they have, what they know and who they are. What does this mean for you? It means you will have to start your work by attending to what is meaningful and valuable to your hosts. After a time, you will be able to go beyond this. But you will be able to do so because you have gained trust and have been able to let them see something new and they have come to value it. It has become important to them and they will work at it with you, not because it is important to you, but because they have decided it is important to them. If you do not take all of the steps, if you convince them to take on something just because it is valuable to you, it probably will not last. To partner and to sometimes lead

will require much trust. How will you gain it? Finally, let me encourage you from this day forward to always look for the good things here. It is easy to get distracted from that. Don't allow anything to make you negative for very long. Keep noticing the good things. There are a great many. Keep discovering them and build on them."

SPECIAL FEATURES

The thoughts that follow are not from Peace Corps literature and do not represent official policy. Rather, they are conclusions reached by watching the Peace Corps at work from a field perspective.

The Peace Corps is recognized as an experience that helps to define one's life and that creates leadership characteristics. Many of the other development organizations that work through volunteers do the same. The Peace Corps has three goals;

1. To promote relevant assistance where requested on challenges jointly identified.

2. To promote understanding of the American people through those serving as volunteers.

3. To promote understanding of others by Americans, through those who have served abroad.

The last goal is one that returned volunteers are supposed to work on throughout life.

A GRASSROOTS ORIENTATION

The approach of the Peace Corps, like other volunteer organizations, is people to people. The idea is that initiatives and efforts are to be jointly owned and managed by host country people and their guests, i.e. Peace Corps volunteers. The Peace Corps, as well as other volunteer organizations, recognize that work done together with their local hosts will be of mutual benefit, not just of benefit to local people. In fact, the case can be made that as much as local people and their institutions gain greatly, perhaps volunteers who have the opportunity to serve gain more. It is the intent of the Peace Corps to address needs most critical to the people of host countries. This does not preclude work on needs of a secondary nature. Given the live in shoulder to shoulder nature of the volunteer approach, it is obvious that volunteer organizations give much credence to development through individual change. Volunteer organizations believe in the problem solving ability of their hosts and work to create conditions for it to be released.

PERSON TO PERSON

The Peace Corps and other volunteer organizations believe in long hours on mutual endeavors. They believe in learning together, making joint plans, and problem solving together. A benefit of this person to person development is a closeness that allows the sharing of aspirations, fears, suspicions, and joys. It contributes to mutual trust and respect, being responsible together, and wanting the best for each other; to becoming one with others.

CONTRIBUTIONS OF VOLUNTEER WORK

Hopefully after two year of close work together, both volunteers and their hosts will be more confident of their own potential, be more open to other's ideas, more amenable to judicious change, more understanding and respectful of different values, more inquisitive about the diverse world, more willing and confident about taking responsibility for themselves, their community, and nation, be more trusting in the manageability of their efforts, more enamored of the benefit of applied skill and hard work, more willing to aspire to new things, be clearer about the demands and opportunities of the world around them, be more caring about people and places – even those far away from home, and be more respectful of the dignity and worth of themselves, others, and of nature. Obviously, to realize the benefits of the one to one approach, volunteer organizations must strive to keep from being imprisoned by their own views, must strive to keep bureaucracy from getting in the way of people to people initiatives, must avoid being prescriptive, must keep the helping relationship central to operations, must promote individual humility, and guard against the arrogance which organizations have a penchant for. The person to person approach offers volunteers an opportunity to experience the vulnerability of the less fortunate, makes volunteers more cognizant of shared humanity, encourages attention to the rights of others and for those who are most reflective, and helps them stay alert to imperatives of the age, e.g. the incremental unification of people's, the manifestation of transcending consciousness, and a growing appreciation of all that unites us.

SINKING DEEP ROOTS

The fact that Peace Corps volunteers have two years to really get involved means they can sink deep roots and work side by side with local people, whether in a government ministry, on a farm, in a school, in a hospital, at a corporate office, in a university, in a conservation district, at a city planning unit, and so on. This person to person approach can be very productive. It can bring about meaningful and sustained change. However, this does not just happen. It requires an understanding of the process. Understandings like the following are important:

– To be effective, those who engage in this kind of development must have credibility.
– Credibility comes from close and long standing association on positive endeavors.
– Change in the complex world of disadvantage comes from pulling with the people.
– People respect those who will see a problem through with them.
– Demonstration and example are more effective than advising.
– Hard challenges require sustained effort.
– Short term cooperation may overlook a host of cultural, social, political, and personal implementation issues.

BELIEF IN PEOPLE

The long term Peace Corps approach that works through side by side partnerships makes it possible for a people to be truly engaged in the planning of their own development and responsible for the change that is desired. This requires them to participate in decision making on goals, approaches, and process. It also requires them to engage wholeheartedly in the work necessary to achievement of goals, once a project or program has been adopted. In work of this nature, it is important to keep in mind that people only sincerely work for what they believe in, that people believe in what they understand as relevant to their needs or the needs of their institution or country. People understand what they can link to previous experiences that they value. Sincere effort happens when someone sees that effort as congruent with what they believe and value. It can be tempting out of courtesy to others for host participants to agree to a goal or an effort that they are less than enthusiastic about. In the interest of a host country's development, it is important that country leaders be aware of the real feelings of those they have chosen to participate in important development efforts. It is also important that local participants be given every opportunity to participate in such a way that they can make a project their own. If that does not happen, a project may achieve a great deal that will not be sustained.

Development specialists are outsiders who have been contracted to achieve things thought to be important. Often what is to be achieved has been planned by experts from abroad in conjunction with host officials. Most things that are to be achieved in accordance with a contract are time bound and quantifiable, i.e. are subject to "as measured by" stipulations. While this can keep work productive, it has to be managed wisely by professionals so that perspective is maintained and so that work remains relevant to true needs as discovered in the process of work. There are several pressures when one is working to a plan and a contract, and it can be tempting to become focused on so called deliverables, to the exclusion of local considerations. The mix of cultures in a development setting can mean there are different views on matters like consultation, decision making, pace of work, quality of work, and even definition of accomplishment. Given the competing pressures, it can be tempting for a development specialist to lose patience with local colleagues, get carried away with the momentum of the development organization to which he or she is contracted, become overly sensitive to themes that are in vogue in the professional development world, give a great deal of credence to so called rich policy research, attempt to move things along with adoption of various technologies, and give undue attention to new thematic thrusts.

It is important that both host country and outside development specialists be aware of these challenges because if an appropriate process is sacrificed to make believe achievement, a development investment can be wasted. Working in person to person development since 1961, the Peace Corps has had extensive experience with these potential dilemmas. Believing in the people of host countries and in its' own volunteers, as well as the person to person approach, the Peace Corps selects personnel, trains volunteers, guides the development process, and works hand in hand with local leaders of every program area to see that success is genuine and sustainable.

BELIEFS HELD BY VARIOUS PROFESSIONALS ABOUT DEVELOPMENTTHAT ARE CONGRUENT WITH THE PEACE CORPS APPROACH

Local level development as the foundation – Many of us in the field of development belief that a nation must function well at the local level in order to work well overall; that initiative, cohesiveness, responsibility, and democratic behavior cannot become a national reality through policy directive, but rather must come about through development of the grass roots. We feel that ultimately, a people must have the capability to help themselves.

Steadfastness – Some of us in development work think that the time needed for significant change is often grossly underestimated. We feel that the complexity of development is often seriously misunderstood; that development entails much more than the making of a plan, plan implementation, and measuring for results. It is thought that steadfast attention to factors beyond those usually looked to is necessary to genuine and sustainable development.

The appropriate level of application – some of us feel it is imperative that participants in development work at levels appropriate to their readiness and preparation, and that trying to accomplish beyond that is futile. That it is necessary to begin with where a people and a society are. It is felt too, that development must proceed at a pace which is realistic and that can be accommodated. We believe it important to employ technologies that can be sustained and that it is critical to work through local institutions and organizations in order that what is accomplished is locally understood and can be sustained.

The appropriate level of resources – we feel too that working outside the capability of a community, institution, or government can create unreal expectations and extreme dependence. We are conscious that accomplishment through local organizations in such a way that they are not meaningfully involved is wasteful and unsustainable. We believe that step by layered step is important to learning and eventual ownership. Unfortunately, it is sometimes precluded by work that is beyond a people's capacity or resources.

These convictions seem to be congruent with the Peace Corps approach. They are no doubt also congruent with the approach of other organizations. The Peace Corps can be a great learning experience. Indeed it can be character building. Volunteers are expected to accomplish complicated and difficult things. However, they have not been made CEO's or project directors. They are partners and advisors. Accomplishment in this situation is all the more admirable. Perhaps that is why former Peace Corps volunteers now fill so many key positions in every type of development organization. Perhaps the Peace Corps experience helps people learn to see the strengths and needs of others. Perhaps it helps them see themselves more clearly. It is probably so that for many, it is an experience that opens them to a deeper appreciation of the world's diversity and leads them to want to stay involved with world issues. It is likely as well, that the Peace Corps experience helps volunteers see and understand interdependencies more clearly, nation to nation, and people to people. In my estimation, the challenging but rewarding Peace Corps experience helps volunteers understand the importance of honest communications, the true sharing of responsibility, cooperative problem solving, empathy, mutual respect, cooperative learning, and trust.

NUTS AND BOLTS OF THE PEACE CORPS

Again, the notes below are not official. Those who become interested in the possibility of making a Peace Corps assignment part of their career can obtain a great deal of information from the Peace Corps website, from publications that can be found in libraries, from books by former volunteers, and from correspondence with regional Peace Corps offices. This said, allow me to briefly touch on the subject.

Support – Generally speaking, the Peace Corps supplies a living allowance, travel costs, medical care and counseling, certain work supplies, emergency leave, medical leave, significant amounts of training, assistance with work planning, assistance with proposal writing, assistance with program evaluations, liaison with government officials (local, district, regional, and national Ministries), housing either directly or with local authorities as part of the host country in-kind contribution, a significant end of service re-adjustment allowance, end of service travel home, assistance on gaining employment, and support of graduate school costs at Universities that are part of the Peace Corps network for this. For example, there are significant opportunities to make one's overseas Peace Corps assignment a simultaneous work and graduate study effort, culminating in a graduate degree at a prestigious university. There are also opportunities to receive financial support to study for a graduate degree, after finishing one's overseas assignment, at a participating university.

Recruitment – The Peace Corps, together with host country institutions and offices, collaboratively identifies development sectors and specific work areas that need guidance and help. Further, the Peace Corps defines specific scopes of work. The Peace Corps determines exact qualifications that a volunteer should have in relation to a scope of work. Offices of the Peace Corps in the US recruit for the position. Upon locating candidates who have appropriate skills and background, the Peace Corps in the US sends information about them to the field Mission. The field mission shares information about a candidate appropriately so that a decision may be made.

Volunteer placement in the field – In collaboration with host country officials, Peace Corps staff members develop sites. For example, they might work with school headmasters, business owners, chamber of commerce officers, information ministry personnel, village leaders, district conservation officers, health clinic administrators, and doctors in hospitals to develop agreements on matters like roles and relationships, the appointment of counterparts, and volunteer accommodations.

Special program assistance – Volunteers who develop proposals on secondary projects have access to financial and other assistance from or through Peace Corps Washington offices.

Specialized training for volunteers – This includes, but is not necessarily limited to, (1) orientation training in Washington (2) orientation with a different emphasis, in the Peace Corps country (3) pre-service training upon arrival in country, conducted over several weeks and covering topics like language, culture, socioeconomic background, legal structure, the economy, in-country resources, Peace Corps/US resources, health, security, and technical subjects related to one's assignment (4) a specialized live in period at a site to get acquainted with local people and their customs (5) the formal swearing in of volunteers in the nation's capital (6) supervisor training whereby local people who will have responsibility toward a volunteer learn about matters like volunteer health services at the Peace Corps, work planning, volunteer and host counterpart responsibilities, volunteer accommodation, Peace Corps provisions for volunteer leave, transport, security, and project characteristics (7) in-service trainings for volunteers periodically that, for example, refresh communication facility, upgrade information system capacities, give information on new research that relates to a volunteer's assignment, and provides information on safety and security (8) an end of service workshop that may last several days and has the purpose of orienting volunteers to life, school, and work at home. The intent is to work with volunteers on a satisfactory re-entry to the U.S. It is probably so that some of the other volunteer organizations have arrangements like this.

OTHER PEACE CORPS POSITIONS AND CAREERS

Organizationally, the Peace Corps is directly under the White House with its Director appointed by the President of the United States. Like other departments of government, there is a certain amount of Congressional oversight. Working with the Director of the Peace Corps are an Assistant Director for Global Operations overseas, three Regional Directors for Africa, Europe, and the Mediterranean, Asia, Inter-America, and the Pacific. Desk Officers for every country guide day to day support to the field. Within Peace Corps headquarters and its regional offices, one finds a great variety of officers, all in some way performing functions that are critical to maintaining a larger organization with a global mission.

Examples of Careers at Peace Corps Washington and at Overseas Missions

There are many career possibilities within the Peace Corps, both at headquarters and at overseas Missions. At headquarters, there are offices responsible for programming support, medical services, volunteer recruitment and selection, staff HR services, research of many types, administrative services, budgets and financial services, training of many types, information technology, overseas transitioning, counseling, legal services, Inspector General work, program evaluation, worldwide facilities, worldwide schools, communications, returned volunteer support, participating university graduate programs, private sector relations and support, field project support, applied research, Peace Corps emergency response operations, international volunteerism, and other matters. This summary of work functions at Peace Corps Washington and its overseas offices is provided to give readers an idea of career possibilities.

Examples of Positions in the Field

The Country Director – In the Country Missions, one finds different staff configurations depending on the country program, the size of the Mission, and other factors. The Country Director for each Mission plans and directs all aspects of the Peace Corps program. He or she ensures day to day operations that create an environment within which volunteers and staff may work successfully. The Country Director is the senior representative of the Peace Corps in the country.

Story Illustrating the Range of Activities of a Country Director

At the sign reading US Peace Corps, the Country Director turned in and drove the long narrow walled lane. Lots of vehicles and bikes were around already this morning. He climbed the stair of the main building. Namaste, Namaste everyone greeted. Some locals added a slight bow with hands together in the respectful position. He returned these polite greetings. He had been away for several days.

Upon his entering the Director's office, Ang Dali came in with a list of phone calls to return. She also presented him with three folders – one of cables from Washington, one of urgent emails and faxes, and one of notes from staff members here at the Country Mission and in the field. When training was in session, there were up to eighty full and part time staff. He turned to his inbox. It was overflowing with letters, many of them from volunteers in the field. There were 144 volunteers in various assignments across the country – some several days away by mountain trail and bus. He received letters from sister organizations of other countries in Nepal and from NGO's and Peace Corps Medical Unit staff.

It was the usual official large brown envelope from the Embassy. Personnel actions to sign, outgoing cables, home of record changes, checks to sign, the cash count to review, a request for early termination, a claim for stolen property, medical hold forms, a medevac to approve urgently, the list of local candidates for an important position, staff work and travel plans, minutes from medical and volunteer security committees, feedback on a grant proposal, a new project plan to review, volunteer assignment descriptions, bids on excess property, a notice of a meeting at USAID, the agenda of this week's Country Team meeting from the Ambassador, an invitation to an official Embassy reception, a request for a speech, a rental contract, a harassment report, letter from a local nursing college; <u>a notice of a missing volunteer</u>. That stopped him! That is what it is all about. His volunteers represent what makes their country great. People like his volunteers make the human race look good. "The selfless work of people like our volunteers, worldwide, helps us triumph over meaner instincts in the world," he thought. And then he read on. The volunteer had been located and there had been no foul *play. He immediately left his office to seek out Tika. "Tika will have the full story," he thought.*

Program and Training Officers – The Programming and Training functions are extremely important. In some Missions they are separate positions and in some they are one. In summary, the person or people who handle these responsibilities plan, lead, and direct programming and training activities for volunteers and sometimes their local counterparts throughout a Peace Corps country. They also supervise multi-cultural training programs for Peace Corps staff. In addition, they assist the Peace Corps Country Director in the administration of the organization, providing supervision, and support to staff and volunteers. Their work involves the assurance of program and training quality, consistent with the needs and interests of the host country. They also engage in the design of evaluations to determine organizational effectiveness. And they work with the Associate Peace Corps Directors (sometimes known as Program Managers) in education, agriculture, conservation, health, business, city planning, or management, etc. to ensure that volunteers make a useful contribution and have a positive professional experience. This means that Associate Peace Corps Directors or Program Officers get involved in every aspect of volunteer work and support from work counseling, to living accommodations, to funding proposals, to security, to professional upgrading, to liaison with various government or private sector entities, to liaison with Peace Corps Washington offices.

Administrative Officers – Each Peace Corps Mission has an Administrative Officer who manages a full range of support functions including budgets and finance, procurement, housing, transportation, safety and security, physical resources, volunteer allowances, communications, records and information systems, HR management, etc. The administrative section of a Peace Corps Mission has well qualified staff for very technical functions.

Medical Officers – Each mission has a chief medical and health officer who is usually a physician. He or she is supported by nurses and other health personnel. The Medical Unit is key to volunteer health, both routine and emergency. It has support from Medical Services at Peace Corps Washington and is connected to designated hospitals around the world. It handles evacuations when necessary and many other matters. It also provides health education and counseling to the volunteer community.

CLOSING THE CHAPTER ON WORKING IN VOLUNTARY DEVELOPMENT ORGANIZATIONS

In closing this chapter, let me leave you with the flavor of the work and the hoped for esprit de corps by sharing a volunteer swearing in ceremony, after new Peace Corps Volunteers have finished their training and are ready to take up field assignments.

The Peace Corps Country Director stood up and walked to the podium. "Honorable Representatives of his Majesty's Government, Madam Ambassador, Distinguished Guests, Peace Corps Staff and Volunteers, Ladies and Gentlemen. Namaste and Welcome. Thank you for coming to these beautiful grounds to celebrate with us.

This is indeed a proud day. Today, 56 Peace Corps Volunteers will be sworn in for service throughout Nepal. They will join 100 other Volunteers already at work here. Over the past decades, many hundreds have served in this astoundingly picturesque Mountain Kingdom. Those who will be sworn in today will work in Education, Water and Sanitation, Nursing, Agriculture, and Community Development. Each of these Volunteers will be answering the call from President John F. Kennedy in 1961 when he challenged the people to "ask not what your country can do for you but what you can do for your country."

I will offer two basic comments today. The first will be addressed to the people of Nepal. The second will be addressed to the Volunteers who have just completed twelve weeks of intensive training in preparation for service to this country.

Citizens and leaders of Nepal – the Peace Corps belongs to all of us. Every Peace Corps project has joint leadership and has an input of resources and labor from your communities. By accepting these American volunteers, you give them a chance to be of assistance to their Nepali brothers and sisters, and in so doing, an opportunity to become better people themselves. As was said many centuries ago, "If anyone would be first, they must be the very last and the servant of all." By accepting these new Volunteers you give them the privilege of living and working side by side with the people of many communities in this country – of sharing in every sense. These Volunteers and their Nepali colleagues are going to have a unique experience over the next two years, an opportunity to learn from each other, time to learn about each other, and to come to know the good in each other. You are opening the door so that these Volunteers may become one with you and may be enriched by Nepal's long history and deep culture.

At the end of each volunteers' tour of service in this country, they should be able to say, like the Roman Senator Seneca, "I was not born for one corner – the world is my native land." The volunteers who will be sworn in here will come to know the richness of the world's diversity. They will learn how critical it is to the future of humanity, to appreciate what other places are and what other people have become.

Ladies and gentleman, by bringing these volunteers to another land, the Peace Corps is acknowledging that the world's people need each other. I don't mean that we need what each other can produce of what we can sell one to another. I mean we need each other. You and I have witnessed unification of the world's people on the physical level. We have indeed become materially interdependent. But the unification is less than well balanced. Orderly, just, and peaceful interdependence will only be possible when we truly know each other. And the knowing of each other will generate respect for other's traditions, values, and characters.

Peace Corps Volunteers – you are about to become engrossed in some of the fundamental matters of our time. You will come to understand a very different place, a people with a history very differ than yours. And as we come to truly know another place and people, that which at a deep level unites a richly diverse species, begins to speak to us. Transcending purpose becomes clear. We become proud of our capacity to practice humanity toward each other. Let this place broaden you and make you a stronger, yet more compassionate human being. And when you leave two years from now, go with Nepal in your hearts.

Finally, volunteers and Nepali counterparts, please remember that as you go about your life and work together, you will be mirrors that when looked into by colleagues, will reflect their dignity and worth. The door stands open for us to exercise the gifts of concern and in so doing, earn a wider citizenship."

Chapter VIII
Working in Health Care

Why do health care organizations engage in the type of work they do? Why do individuals prefer to work in one kind of development over another? What might you consider when deciding on the kind of work you will train for and engage in? The chapter that follows emphasizes approaches in development health care. Each is vital. They are not mutually exclusive. There are common and overlapping features.

Complementary Efforts

Hands on Action

In this, direct work, e.g. research, treatment, and so on, is emphasized. The building of local capacity is considered important but direct engagement and responsibility is the paramount objective. This is quite consistent with strict project assistance where development personnel operate quite independently with project resources that their home company or agency controls. Often they offer specialized services that are unavailable in the host country. Projects of this kind operate in accordance with meticulously defined objectives and targets of achievement. Inputs and actions are time sensitive. They are routinely monitored and evaluated against agreed upon objectives and quality standards. They are accountable to their source of funding but of course in keeping with host country policy. The mission is clear and limited. An example of this would be a multi-nation campaign, over a period of years, to eliminate a major illness.

Capacity Development

In this, the building of local capacity is emphasized. Direct services are not put aside but the intent is to accomplish them through a partnership of local and international effort. The development of local capacity is very important. This is quite consistent with program assistance where technical specialists or advisors combine efforts with local leadership and professional specialists. The idea is to engage the host country and host institutions in such a way that locally identified needs are addressed with both local and international resources and that local capacity and commitment is improved along the way. While developing health solutions and performing medical services, it is planned to develop local skills, change unproductive operations and behaviors, build local confidence and the sense of ownership, increase management capabilities, reform systems, organizations, and policies, and work in such a way that achievements are sustained.

Obviously the selection of an approach has to be made based on a country's readiness, the urgency of a health problem, the philosophy of agencies and donors, and whether inadequate or inappropriate health services seem to be a product of customs, organization, and management or the actual level of expertise in a country's health establishment.

Context

For context, let us start this chapter with some important facts. These relate to a significant portion of the health situation in the developing world.

While a great deal of progress has been made in the health of millions, much is still to be done. The health situation of rich and poor worldwide is significantly different. The status of women versus men in many parts of the world denies opportunities that have an impact on women's health. And given the role of women in the family everywhere in the world, whole families can be affected by a mother's situation. For example, what a family raises for consumption, a family's nutrition, the habits of children regarding hygiene, a family's sleep routine, and the encouragement of children with respect to work and school is largely dependent on aware and responsible mothers.

Some people in developing countries live in extremely unhealthy or unsafe environments, both urban and rural. Many families have an income insufficient to allow professional health care. Over 95% of the childhood deaths in the world occur in poor countries. There is a startling difference between the richest 20% and the poorest 20% in terms of mortality rates under the age of five.

The soaring rate of HIV infection has dealt a devastating blow in some poor countries. Nearly two thirds of HIV positive people live in African countries. There are some countries where nearly one third of the population caries the disease. Life expectancy in Sub-Saharan Africa has declined in the last few years and is in the neighborhood of 47 to 50% because of this.

Child mortality has declined in low to middle income counties but over ten million children still die each year, many from diseases that could be treated with existing approaches if resources, expertise, or social conditions were different. Unfortunately, the rate of improvement in child health in many countries is declining. This decline is most noticeable in countries which already have the highest child mortality.

Adding to sicknesses that have traditionally affected millions, certain chronic diseases are on the increase in developing countries, e.g. cardiovascular diseases, obesity, cancer, diabetes, and respiratory diseases.

Surely, the challenge remains great. However, there have been very significant successes from international health interventions in recent decades. Overall, life expectancy in the developing world has increased quite dramatically. Polio in Latin America has largely been defeated. River Blindness in huge parts of Africa is under control, women in parts of South Asia almost never die in child birth anymore, Small Pox has been eliminated, Tuberculosis in China has been dramatically reduced – and Trachoma, the leading cause of preventable blindness in North Africa, has been greatly slowed amongst children. There are more examples of success in the developing world through the efforts of intrepid heath care professionals.

So, while the challenges remain large, there is significant promise in even the poorest of countries. By changing behaviors, and by applying new technologies, the professional health community has been able to make great strides. Realizing that development is ultimately an integrated endeavor, for example that customs, income, the distribution of resources, the efficiencies of government, and gender and ethnic opportunity all play a role in the possibility for good health, there is no doubt that the development community's broad efforts, in conjunction with the specific interventions of health care specialists, can make much more headway.

Hands on Action

As indicated on the first page of this chapter, some who enter the field of development health care, will choose to be engaged in direct action. They will be professionals in disease research or pharmaceutical development, project implementers, institutional administrators, doctors, nurses, medical technologists, health care educators, nutritionists and so on. In large measure they will operate through projects that have donor or agency support and which lend themselves to carefully targeted campaign like efforts.

System Capacity Development

Others will be of assistance regarding customs and behaviors, advocacy and public education, governmental reform and reorganization, legal frameworks and processes that need to be developed or refined, revenue arrangements that should to be improved, health systems that have to function better, communities that need to focus on helping their populations, political parties that should to be made aware of social disparities, and perhaps most importantly, initiatives to accompany developments so that whatever is achieved will be sustained, that is, will not go away once the formal development effort has been finished.

How might developing nation governments, interest groups, and development organizations take on the challenge of further building systems that result in much improved health care?

To really speak to this would necessitate writing a book. But let me briefly outline some points because they are important to anyone considering a career in health care. They help to put the challenge into a system perspective.

First – in any particular country or region, an assessment of the present system together with the society that supports it needs to be undertaken. An outline of a methodology to kick this off might be discussions by numerous professionals and citizen groups to:

a) think through the strengths of the present system, e.g. advantages, experience, unique characteristics, resources, competence, capabilities, quality, and reputation.

b) think through the weaknesses of the present system, e.g. disadvantages, gaps in knowledge and expertise, resources, reliability, trust, ability to attract, and keep good personnel.

c) think through strengths versus weaknesses.

d) think through opportunities for moving ahead, e.g. strategic alliances, partnerships, availability of resources, willingness of communities and individuals to engage and support.

e) think through threats to reform and improvement efforts, e.g. vested interests that might feel at risk, loss of alliances or partners, aiming beyond what is doable, and getting involved with the wrong advisors or organizations.

f) think through each topic, i.e. strengths, weaknesses, opportunities and threats, and write preliminary goals.

Second – from this an identification of the new conditions that need to be achieved would be stated.

Third – a detailed blueprint of actions for bringing about these conditions would be developed.

Fourth – resources that might be able to support an integrated and comprehensive development effort would be identified.

Fifth – a request would be made that organizations which have an interest in an effort to accomplish the blueprint, put forth ideas on how they would proceed.

Sixth – an organization to work with the developing country on the project would be selected.

Seventh – a framework clearly mapping the proposed effort would be developed, i.e. purpose, goals, outputs, actions, means of verification, and work plans.

Hands on Action

Some who enter the field of development health care will choose to become professionals in disease research or pharmaceutical development, project implementers, institutional administrators, doctors, nurses, medical technologists, health care educators, nutritionists, and so on, who work on campaign like projects which have donor or agency funding and which are tightly planned and targeted to limited and time sensitive objectives.

Examples of positions in this kind of health care development might be:

Project Directors, Senior Physicians, Nursing Coordinators, Nutrition Coordinators, Staff Developers, Mentoring and Training Coordinators, Maternal and Child Health Specialists, Family Planning Specialists, HIV and Tuberculosis Specialists, Health Budget and Accounting Specialists, Lifestyle Specialists, Clinical Trials Coordinators, Senior Epidemiologists, Behavioral and Social Sciences Specialists, Laboratory Technologists, Biostatisticians, Data Management Specialists, Medical Writers, Research Associates, Quality Assurance Specialists, Malaria, Dengue Fever and Influenza Specialists, Biologists, Emergency Response Specialists, Behavioral Scientists, Health Education Specialists, Health Information/Communications Specialists, Medical Officers, Public Health Analysts, Public Health Advisors, Audio Visual Production Specialists, Computer Information Technology Specialists, Human Resources Specialists, Program Managers, Biologists, Microbiologists, Contracts and Grants Specialists, Engineers, Public Affairs Specialists, and Statisticians.

Capacity Development

Others will undertake to be of assistance regarding customs and behaviors, advocacy, public education, governments that need to reorganize, legal frameworks and processes that need to be developed or refined, revenue arrangements that need to be made or changed, health systems that need to function better, communities that need to focus on helping their populations, political parties that need to be made aware of social disparities, and perhaps most importantly, initiatives that need to accompany developments so that whatever is achieved will be sustained. Examples of positions in this kind of healthcare development might be:

Chiefs of Party, Senior Physician Specialists, Senior Nursing Specialists, Directors of Administration, Directors of Planning and Evaluation, Systems Planners, Directors of Training, Directors of Public Education, Advocacy Specialists, Legal Reform Specialists, Revenue Generation and Equalization Advisors, Centralization and Decentralization Specialists, Institutional Capacity Specialists, Behavioral Change and Communications Specialists, Private Sector Cooperation Specialists, Coordinators of Work with Government Ministries, Social and Community Mobilization Specialists, Coordinators of Work with other Health Projects, Coordinators of Cooperative Endeavors with NGO's, Institutional Strengthening Specialists, Advisors to Unit Directors at Health and other Ministries, Advisors to Unit Directors at Health Institutions and Health Management Information Systems Advisors.

ANOTHER KIND OF HEALTH CARE DEVELOPMENT

As with any sophisticated endeavor, work in the field of health care mixes cognitive effort with human affective capacity. Let us get into what one may encounter in the field, in ways other than technical. This too is important to those who are struggling with decisions about a career.

The mix of what a person is or what a people are can be a fascinating challenge; sometimes a puzzle. My guess is that the more one is curious about other people and admires the fact that the human race has many intriguing cultures, the easier it is to deal with this dimension. Those who work in health care get closer to other human beings than perhaps any other profession. Understanding patients, or even research populations, can make a significant difference in outcome. The thing is, patients like all people, differ greatly. A patient might exhibit certain characteristics because of illness of course. They may be easy or difficult to deal with because of illness. But other factors enter in, e.g. belief systems, personality, socioeconomic class, level of education, age, gender, ethnicity, language spoken, level of trust based on previous experiences, sense of belonging, general awareness, and urban or rural background. All of these variations are made more complicated by one's culture. Knowing how powerful culture is in a life may lead many of us to ascribe certain things to it that are really a less complicated phenomenon. In any event, this presents a fascinating yet sometimes life and death challenge. It is a land where stereotype can take over when in fact, it may not apply. Everyone is unique and when you consider how many of us there are, this is daunting from a responsibility for health care perspective.

Some Examples

A woman who abhors complaint, does not make her physician know how sick she is and dies. What or who is responsible for this? Her personality, a stern father, her gender, her difficulty with the doctor's language, mistrust, or deep cultural factors? In a way it does not matter. What matters is that the doctor did not understand. Working in a foreign setting makes this all the more vexing.

A man whose culture believes it can be dangerous for a sick person to learn how ill they are because it can destroy hope, is told candidly that he is very sick by a western physician. She does this as a matter of course because it is convention in her country to level with patients. The patient gets much sicker unnecessarily.

A woman who practices traditional relaxation through meditation and the burning of herbs on her back, sees a project physician for depression. In the course of diagnosis he discovers scars on the patient's back and decides she is subject to marital abuse.

A woman who visits a project clinic makes no eye contact whatsoever. The male counselor there determines that she is seriously depressed. In fact, in her culture it would be very inappropriate for someone of her station to make eye contact with any male other than her husband. In some cultures this would happen because it would suggest sexual impropriety, or that one is insuring not to lose their soul. In some cultures even to take a picture of someone is to steal their soul.

Clinic personnel may believe in the importance of comforting touch. However, in some cultures touch, other than for hands on care, is prohibited.

Concluding that a patient refuses assistance with a medical condition because of culture when in fact, the reason may be as simple as cost.

Complications do not have to be related to physical care of course. I recall a highly educated local professional who was employed to gather data, analyze it, and write a report. Even though she seemed to know the task well, it never happened. There was always an excuse. Perhaps her supervisor was expecting her to ask culturally inappropriate questions and she was embarrassed to reveal that.

There are many factors that will have to be the subject of further investigation by the reader. Answers may be different for each culture in which one works. Subjects of investigation that might be helpful include getting into a culture, personal space, listening, pecking order, power and influence, being a woman, men's work, women's work, modesty, motivation for working, crossing bridges of confidence, not giving offence, embarrassing others, the detrimental effect of having a credential, and so on.

CULTURE AND MEDICINE
Two Actual Incidents

The Healer

It must be that people in town are used to seeing Jacob around. Otherwise he could have been in big trouble this morning when folks on the footpath along the Kingsway saw a white guy pull up to a teenaged Mosotho girl and insistently urge her to get into his car – finally getting out and shoving her in. Who would know her to be his maid's daughter and that the girl, Mantua, does not know where she is again today. These walkabouts are an awful worry to Me' Agatha. This afternoon, Agatha's friend Elsie practically sat on Mantua in the maid's quarters. Fortunately her size, her loud laughing, and antics calmed Mantua. Late this afternoon, Agatha convinced Jacob to drive them out to the healer on the Roma road again. When they got ready to leave the healer's, Mantua was quietly seated in a circle with other women on the packed earth of the little building. Each was dressed in a white gown. The healer was wearing a red robe. Mantua had her little vial of water with her. She seemed happy and contented to stay behind. If all goes well, she will get back to balance and they will pick her up day after tomorrow. Me' Agatha, who was distraught about her daughter, is relieved to have Mantua with the healer.

The Taker

This afternoon a small tan car parked on their narrow dirt street for several hours. A man dressed in a blue blanket sat behind the wheel surveying the neighborhood. Periodically, Jacob and Agatha checked the window to see what he might be doing. After a time, they noticed he had called a small boy over. The little boy, Rapheli, often comes to their door for sweets. Then they saw Rapheli get into the car. Jacob immediately left the house. "Do you know this boy Ntate?" Jacob asked the stranger. The driver had obviously been drinking.

"Yes, he is a friend."

"Do you know this man Rapheli?" Jacob asked the small boy.

"No, Ntate, I don't know him."

The man continued to look down. "Do you know me, the stranger asked?"

"No," Jacob said.

"Maybe I don't want you to know me," the man said.

"Where does the boy live?" Jacob asked. The man pointed to the wrong house. Jacob asked Rapheli where he lived and he pointed in the opposite direction.

"You don't like me," the driver said, "I am just a blanket man." Jacob told him that Rapheli is a friend and that he is a good boy. In blurred words the man replied, "This boy has something I envy here," circling Rapheli's head with his finger. "He is a brilliant boy."

Recalling stories about ancient practices here and remembering that although outlawed, some of it apparently still goes on, Jacob became alarmed. "I must take the boy home to his mother, she will be wondering where he is," Jacob said.

The man said in a cold tone, "I'll take him tnere," again pointing in the wrong direction. Jacob nodded and the man edged his car ahead. It was a dead end, a wall just ahead. Jacob continued to stand in the narrow street and Rapheli got out. *This guy will have to get his medicine some other way, if that is what he is after*, Jacob thought.

The above stories were taken from the author's experiences.

HEALTH AND WELL BEING PLANNING

Healthy Living for Youth
The Case of Jordan

There is another kind of development health care. In fact, it is sort of a healthcare plus because it involves other disciplines and works across sectors. Rather than being targeted on a disease or a patient, it is targeted on a group. It in fact addresses the welfare of a group from several perspectives, e.g. the group's education, its mental and physical health, opportunities open to it, the economy that supports it, negative and positive influences, the society surrounding it, the group's cultural foundations, the changing world within which the group lives, and the preparations the group needs to make in order to cope and hopefully thrive. One might decide that this kind of endeavor is fascinating and worthy. Hence they might prepare themselves to do health research or health planning, integrated national and regional policy development, national socioeconomic planning, or the development of wide view campaigns for NGO advocacy groups as ways to get into it. Let us take a group (the youth of Jordan) and work this through.

Following are suggestions for action that could further promote healthy lifestyles for Jordan's youth. Health for this example is defined broadly, encompassing physical, emotional, and social characteristics. Because proposed actions fall mainly in the sphere of promotion through education, it is noted that this is already seen as an important educational responsibility in Jordan. While a great deal has been written on health, in education circles, it is instructive to go to a foundation document for guidance on what is fundamentally intended for Jordan's youth. Relevant excerpts from the Education Act in Jordan are noted here.

Article 9 - The Basic Education Cycle

This cycle aims at realizing the general objectives of education and preparing the citizen in all aspects of his personality; physical, mental, social, and spiritual so that he shall be able to:

1) Care for his environment's safety, purity, beauty, and resources.

2) Realize the importance of his health and physical fitness and practice suitable healthy activities.

Article 11 - The Secondary Education Cycle

This cycle aims at building up a citizen who shall be able to:

1) Adapt to environmental variables related to his or her homeland and to its natural, demographic, social, and cultural dimensions, as well as to work towards investing, maintaining, improving, and developing his or her potential.

2) Preserve the environment and its cleanliness and develop its potential and wealth.

3) Assimilate and apply health information and rules pertaining to balanced physical and psychological growth.

Because the health of a people is dependent on the health of the society and environment within which they live, and because the health of a society is dependent on the health of its people, the section which follows is written from a broad interrelated perspective.

THE CONTEXT IN WHICH JORDAN'S YOUTH LIVE AND FUNCTION

Understanding the Jordanian context is important to understanding the opportunities and challenges that its youth face. Jordan has done very well for its people. However, as with any country, there remain serious challenges. The following analysis presents a picture of the situation within which the health of the nation's youth, in the broadest sense, is born, nurtured, challenged, and lives. In terms of ordinary basic indicators, Jordan's progress is as follows.

In infant mortality, defined as the probability of dying between birth and five years of age, expressed per 1000 live births, Jordan ranks as number 95 out of 193 countries. That is, it is between number 193 Sweden, and number 1 in infant mortality, Sierra Leone. This of course is good. On the other hand it challenges the country to maintain what it has accomplished and to continue to improve.

With respect to the infant mortality rate, Jordan has improved tremendously since 1960. It had a rate of just 27 such deaths per thousand births in 2002 compared to its rate of infant mortality in 1960 of 97. Incidentally, Jordan's rate of 27 in 2002 compares with 46 for the Middle East and North Africa as a whole, 99 for the group of countries known as least developed, 5 for the so called industrialized world, and with 58 for the world as a whole. Jordan has progressed well but of course must be vigilant lest it slip back.

The country has a fairly high birth rate. This has implications in terms of the opportunities it must somehow create for its youth. It has implications for the nature of its responsibility in citizen care and well-being, in the broadest sense. The annual population birth rate is approximately 28 per 1000 people. This is down from 50 some 30 years ago. It compares with 27 for the Middle East and North Africa as a whole, with 39 for the least developed countries, with 12 for the industrialized world and with 22 for the world as a whole. The country is not large and it has limited resources. At the moment it is obviously much less crowded than some others, e.g. Egypt, India, and Pakistan. Living for the most part is pleasant and healthful. The environment has not been severely over taxed by population. But the rate of growth through birth is relatively high and the carrying capacity in this dry land is a question.

Jordan has a particular challenge related to continuing to develop and maintain healthy living through services and opportunities in urban areas. Urban Jordan is growing at a rate of 4.9% per year. This compares with 3% for the Middle East and North Africa, with 4.7% for the least developed countries, with 0.8 % for the industrialized world, and with 2.4 % for the world as a whole. Surely the environment, the possible style of living, and the mental and physical health of its citizens is challenged by rapid urbanization. Looking at one resource alone, it is sobering that Jordan's use of water is 104% of its annual renewable resources. Its extraction or mining of groundwater is almost 180% of its renewable base. Population growth and urbanization are contributing to economic opportunities in the short term but present serious long term socioeconomic and health challenges.

Success often brings new challenges. For example, Jordan has obviously worked hard to make life better. Life expectancy stands at 71, up from 54 some thirty years ago. This compares with 67 for the Middle East and North Africa as a whole, with 49 for the least developed countries, with 78 for the industrialized countries, and with a world average of 63. It is a measure of success and of well-being. But of course, it presents maintenance challenges as well.

Still considering the broader context for populace well-being and for opportunity and health amongst the nation's youth, it is instructive to examine some basic economic indicators. The gross national income per capita in Jordan for 2002 was 1,760 US dollars. This compares with 1,359 for the Middle East and North Africa as a whole, with 277 for the least developed countries, with 26,214 for the industrialized countries, and with a world average of 5,073. Clearly Jordan is doing well compared to many others. But affording some of the social and health services any nation needs for its youth is not an easy matter.

As another picture of the general context within which Jordan's youth are living, developing, and preparing for the future, let us consider education. The nation's adult male literacy stands at 95%, up from 90% ten years ago. Jordan is doing well. This compares with 74% for the Middle East and North Africa as a whole, with 62% for the least developed countries and with a world average of 84%. The literacy rate for adult females is outstanding as well. In the year 2000, it stood at 84% compared to 52 % for the Middle East and North Africa, with 42% for the least developed countries and with a world average of 74%. Given its gross national income per capita, it is quite remarkable that Jordan has achieved this. It has obviously given the education of its people high priority. It is known that education correlates highly with health and well-being. For example, a literate mother is much more likely to have healthy, well-nourished children who practice reasonable hygiene. A literate mother and father are much more likely to open the doors of opportunity for their children. An educated family is more likely to have a livable income and its children are more likely to have a healthy self-image, confidence, and enterprising behaviors. However, there is a challenge for a nation that has well educated people and limited resources. Well educated people look for good fulfilling jobs. Not finding them can be emotionally debilitating and perhaps even physically difficult. While it is certainly a good thing to have a well educated population, keeping employment for them is a serious responsibility.

The context of well-being for Jordan's youth has obviously received considerable attention in the formal education sector. For example, the net primary school enrolment in Jordan (being the number of children enrolled compared to the total children in the primary schooling age group) was 93% for boys and 94% for girls in 2000. This compares with 63% for boys and 58% for girls in the Middle East and North Africa, with 67% for boys and 61% for girls in the least developed countries, 96 % for boys and 97% for girls in the industrialized countries, and with 85% for boys and 79% for girls in the world as a whole.

Moving from the broader context to indicators that more specifically represent conditions of health, it is interesting to note that the percentage of children born with a low birth weight in Jordan is 10. This compares with 15% in the Middle East and North Africa, with 18% in the least developed countries, 7% in the industrialized countries, and 16% in the world at large.

Another fairly direct indicator of health conditions for a nation's youth is the percentage of a population that uses improved drinking water. In the year 2000, this was 84% in Jordan's rural areas, whereas it was 77% in the rural parts of the Middle East and North Africa, 55% in the rural parts of the least developed countries, and 71% for the rural parts of the world at large. Given the water resources of the Middle East and of Jordan in particular, it will be a serious challenge to maintain this standard.

Some other indicators of health, in the broadest sense, for Jordan's youth are as follows:

Rural population using adequate sanitation facilities:

Jordan	98%
Middle East and North Africa	70%
Least developed countries	35%
Industrialized countries	100%

Expanded immunization vaccine application funded by government:

Jordan	100%
Middle East and North Africa	70%
Least developed countries	54%

Adult HIV prevalence (ages 15-49)

Jordan	0.1%
Middle East and North Africa	0.4%
Least developed countries	1.4%
Industrialized countries	0.3%
World average	1.2%

Life expectancy of females as a percentage of male life expectancy:

Jordan	103%
Middle East and North Africa	105%
Least developed countries	104%
Industrialized countries	108%
World average	105%

Percentage of women (aged 15-49) in union, who use contraception:

Jordan	56%
Middle East and North Africa	52%

Least developed countries	27%
Industrialized countries	74%
World average	60%

Percentage of women (aged 15-49) attended at least once during pregnancy by skilled health care personnel:

Jordan	96%
Middle East and North Africa	66%
Least developed countries	55%
World average	70%

While Jordan is doing well within its region, the discussion above would indicate that it has some special challenges related to providing a healthy environment of opportunity for its youth. These are related to the growth of overall population, rapid urbanization, the carrying capacity of its environment, e.g. its land and its water resources, and maintaining income opportunities that are suitable to young people's needs.

CONCERNS ON THE MINDS OF JORDAN'S YOUTH

While the challenges growing out of the facts above should be on everyone's mind, not everyone may be aware of them or if they are, may not have realized how they relate to the continuing well-being of the nation's youth. However, there are very definitely social, health, and economic well-being concerns on the minds of the nation's young people. In 2002 a national study entitled, Jordanian Youth: Their Lives and Views was published by UNICEF. It was based on interviews with approximately 7500 young people. For purposes of the study, the age group 10 to 25 was considered youth. Some of the findings that speak to the social, health, and economic well-being of the nation's youth, in the broadest sense are these:

Youth and Employment

Over 30 percent of the population in Jordan is classified as youth by the definition above. Bearing in mind that youth between 15 and 19 years of age live in a variety of circumstances, some of them still studying full time, some part time and some out of school, it is still of interest to note that over 95% of females in this age group do not work. Of the males in this age group, about 30% work. In the next age group, i.e. between 20 and 24, about 10% of the females are employed. For males this figure is somewhat over 50%. Having so many unemployed at these ages is something that may have long range implications for individuals and the nation. Of those who do work, most like their jobs, although most also are quite dissatisfied with their income. It would seem that the phenomenon of so many young people not being in work situations should be seriously looked into in terms of things like long term self-esteem, potential for entrepreneurship, personal confidence, self-reliance, participation in society, and long term stability.

Youth and Education

Education is popular in Jordan. Boys see it somewhat differently than girls though. For many boys, education is a route to job opportunities. For girls it is more likely to be something one does for its intrinsic value. While education is popular for many, there is some thought that education should be more practical and should be offered in ways that contribute more to things like personal development, self-awareness and confidence, problem solving abilities, and anchored more firmly to the challenges of life in the world of work. Given the present employment challenges in Jordan together with the rapidly growing youth population, this is in a broad sense, a social, health, and economic well-being issue.

Youth and Social Participation

Mobility helps to determine one's ability to participate in the components of life. In every society there are restrictions on this for a variety of reasons. In Jordan, girls have more mobility restrictions than boys. However, this is not a clear and easily understood issue. Other factors enter in such as socioeconomic status, age, and level of education. There is a seeming dilemma with regard to participation in society across the gender divide. Young people express a desire to be more involved socially and in civil society but yet are not confident about doing so. Over three quarters of those surveyed thought that young people should participate more actively in decision making at home, at school and college, at work, and in their communities. Yet when one looks at the rate of involvement in vehicles that could facilitate participation, it is obvious that only 7.6% participate in student councils, 5.3% participate in a sports clubs, with much smaller percentages in other organizations. Jordan needs its youth to become resourceful and confident because to thrive and be stable, every country counts on public responsibility and initiative. Also, engaged individuals are more likely to be psychologically healthy. In terms of maturation, it is natural in a free situation, for the youngest and least mature to be focused on what is closest to them with a focus on and commitment to ever widening concerns as they mature. This is good for society and good for individuals.

Youth and Their Parents

Even though schooling in Jordan has a very traditional base, young people have increasingly been exposed through school and through Jordan's on-going process of economic and social development to new concepts of democracy, gender equality, decision making, and other issues. Families are close and respect across the generations is admirable. Yet there is an apparent difference in perceptions and opinions between the generations. It is natural in every society that parental influence decreases as children grow older. But perhaps in Jordan, something more is gradually happening. If in fact young people are gaining increased jurisdiction in their lives, then perhaps there are things that should be put into place to make them better prepared for this. Indeed, perhaps this is something that should be brought into the open so as to be dealt with in a healthy way by families and society.

Youth and Citizenship

Jordanian society is quite open to the world. And within, it is more and more participatory. According to the survey, young people have a fairly good impression of their communications and human relations capabilities. And many are apparently quite aware of human rights issues. But of course, participatory citizenship is demanding of personal characteristics that go beyond this. Healthy democratic participation is tied to other issues. There needs to be congruence between personal values and ways of being as well as organizational values and ways of being if individuals and the organizations of which they are part are to function in a healthy and productive manner. This is so of course for entire countries.

Youth and Personal Mind Set

It is common for young people anywhere to be tentative, somewhat confused, and lacking in confidence. After all, they are at the beginning of life and have a lot to sort out. In the study, the impression of youthful confusion, lack of confidence in the future, lack of aspiration, inability to take initiative, ambivalence about roles, and apathy is quite prevalent.

Youth and Smoking

It is reported that some young people begin smoking as early as ten years of age. Seven out of ten young Jordanians know of peers who smoke. Children are targeted by tobacco companies that distribute cigarettes outside movie houses and other public places. Smoking among the young is a serious problem in the country.

ACTION FOR WHICH THE DATA CALLS

This analysis suggests the importance of confronting youth with facts in such a way that true understanding results, a sense of personal responsibility is engendered, and healthy constructive behaviors are generated and displayed in relation to:

1) Population growth

2) Reproductive behavior

3) Stewardship toward the environment, i.e. caring for Jordan's air, its land, and its water

4) Consumption, preservation, wastefulness, and sharing

5) Being responsible about educational opportunities

6) Being responsible and honest about the opportunity to work, e.g. wishing to excel, being productive, taking initiative, accepting responsibility, and being honest.

7) Participating in civil society in the interest of one's fellow citizens and the country, e.g. in charities, volunteer groups, development organizations, local government, NGO's, and in service clubs.

8) Being discerning, respectful and committed to fairness, equal opportunity, dialogue and understanding across genders, families, the very old and very young, the disabled and disadvantaged.

9) Willingness to understand other viewpoints, to genuinely listen, to speak honestly, and to promote truth, fairness, and reconciliation.

10) Willingness to take care of the gift of life, e.g. to exercise, to eat properly, to refrain from smoking, and to refrain from other harmful substances.

11) Determination to help others, e.g. those who have health problems, those who have substance abuse problems, those who are discriminated against, and those who are unemployed.

This then is a look at health and the factors which influence it. Perhaps it is professional work that you might find interesting.

---

1. *Figures in this chapter were taken from a study by the author on Jordan in 2004.*

140

141

Chapter IX
Justice and Development
Working for Fairness, Equal Opportunity and a
Stable Peace

Justice Necessary to Development

It is felt by many that justice – being the ability of ordinary citizens to claim rights and resources peacefully and to live within a responsible system of accountable government that listens to and respects the will of the people, and having access to the rule of law in support of economic activity with equal opportunity – is a necessary condition for the development of a people and their nation.

Development Supportive of Justice

It is also felt by many that development – being a condition where citizens have education adequate to living a productive and responsible life, where they have the conditions necessary to health, and where all have the fundamental necessities of life – is supportive of justice.

Context

While great strides have been made toward justice and development in significant areas of the world, both are still lacking in other places around the globe. It is said that several billion people live without significant rights, without access to protection of the law, and are vulnerable to violence, exploitation, and the loss of their property. Indeed, we have seen the poor who live in shacks forced to move so that wealthy condominiums might be erected. We have seen wealthy vacation homes established on public waterways that had been for all people, it being said that city fathers were paid off by developers. Several billion of the world's poorest are at a disadvantage in dealing with criminal or civil justice systems that others are able to use for protection.

Fairness and justice are fundamental to equitable and sustainable development. But even where equity is protected by law, the very poorest often cannot afford to access it. Ordinary citizens need to be able to claim their rights under the law peacefully, and to be able to hold those who represent them accountable to law. It is not uncommon for the poorest to be victims of labor abuse, to be denied appropriate compensation and even information on their rights. Farmers who have insufficient resources often cannot defend themselves against land grabs. Ordinary traders are sometimes not able to do business because they are unable to pay bribes demanded by the police. People who live in slums are often unable to access the justice system of their own city to keep industry from polluting their water.

Many people simply live with this, knowing that one day it will catch up to them by making their children sick. Teachers and other public servants in some jurisdictions keep their jobs by laboring on the public purse for rich politicians, i.e. doing the work of a favored few at the expense of those who pay the taxes. In some places it happens that those who get themselves into trouble because of their poverty are removed because they are a bother to those with power by becoming victims of police crossfire when raids are supposedly made on serious criminals. In some places, people with meager resources are not able to pay the bribes that would get their children into school or their parents into the hospital. I have been impressed by the work of garment workers in Asia, only to find that after work many sleep on the earth behind a factory. We could go on but the point has been made.

Unless justice can somehow be made accessible to all equitably, people will remain disadvantaged and their nations will remain undeveloped, or developed only for a minority.

And unless nations can become at least somewhat developed, the wherewithal of civilization, i.e. education, healthcare, public infrastructure, and so on that would allow citizens to flourish, will not be available and justice will remain an unaffordable luxury.

LET US TAKE AN EXAMPLE

An insurgency took root in western Nepal in the early 1990's based on long standing disadvantage and inequity. By 1996 it had spread across the nation. The insurgency destroyed villages, communities, and families and left a scar on the people nationwide. It is accepted that the insurgency was able to take hold because of very serious inequities and high poverty rates among the poor. As is often the case, indigenous nationalities (known as Janjatis) and those born into low caste (Dalits) were especially unable to move upward, and were stuck in abject poverty. Under certain conditions, class can be transcended but caste is a much harder thing to leave. Districts most affected were at the bottom of development indices. Clearly, lack of justice and opportunity were seeds of the insurgency. As well, lack of development among the poorest was a condition that inhibited just and equitable living.

Also, unequal development in rich areas versus isolated and disadvantaged regions brought great envy and exacerbated the feeling of being forgotten and discriminated against. This inflamed the insurgency. Disadvantaged regions and villages became increasingly poor and isolated. Hence they could not, for example, attract teachers and could not keep them at work when they did attract them. These regions became so demoralized and anarchic that government officials posted there were rarely at their posts. This further fueled the insurgency which in turn discouraged commerce and caused local businesses to flounder. Given the degenerating conditions, traditional traders and livestock herders could not maintain their work. The areas affected became lawless. Bribery and other coercion became rampant. The weakest were taken advantage of, pushed off their land, lost their grazing rights, and were excluded from community forestry groups. There was a downward spiral of a region and a people that the world did not notice for a considerable time. Governance became almost impossible. The little infrastructure that existed was seriously damaged. Local institutions were destroyed and civilians were extorted and forced to support (or even fight for) one side or the other. The traditional limitations on the roles of women made things even more difficult. Many of the young gradually took sides, thinking something had to be done. Hence, some families became divided and certainly whole villages became divided. As time moved on, each side was polarized, becoming more or less home to different ethnic groups.

For those who looked ahead to an eventual end to strife, after everyone became exhausted and decimated, the road to peace and rebuilding looked bleak. The seriously disadvantaged region that took up arms against those in other parts of the nation whose lives were not as futile, slowly turned against itself, family against family, neighbor against neighbor, and social group against social group.

The most enlightened of the country hoped against hope that one day a sort of peace would get a beachhead and ever so slowly open the door for humanitarian relief, the rebuilding of individual confidence, the re-establishment of family cohesiveness, community cooperation, infrastructure repair, the return of government services, and a renewal of business investment.

Peace would not automatically eliminate lingering grievances and without the skillful repair of fundamental conditions, things would ultimately come apart again.

As with any serious conflict area, the end of war in Nepal would leave social marginalization in place and leave old problems intact like economic disparity, gender discrimination, illiteracy, disease, landlessness, malnourishment, orphan-hood, and homelessness. Without the establishment of at least some amount of social justice, development would not happen. And without at least some amount of economic development, justice for those who had been left behind for generations could not become real. It would be a difficult road.

Somehow, people's fear and distrust, caused by both sides when kidnapping, property destruction, killing, torture, and detention were practiced, would need to be addressed if neighbors would ever be able to face each other again and if community institutions would ever become viable again. Displaced and disenfranchised people, together with alienated communities, would need to be brought together with everyone else. Otherwise accomplishments would be shallow, partial, and temporary.

Somehow, people would need to be engaged in such a way that they would work side by side again. But this would not be easy given the understandable abundance of cynicism, fear, and fatalism that had accumulated.

If you were engaged as a consultant what would your advice be? Better yet, what specific interventions would you plan?

This description of the dilemma in Nepal at the time, gives a picture that is in part misleading. It is easy to think of failing states as unattractive and miserable. This is not necessarily so. It certainly has not been the norm for Nepal, this beautiful country in the high Himalayas on top of the world. Let me paint a picture for you.

Staring down on us in silence...seemingly a stone's throw but actually twelve miles distant...
Intimidating snow dressed Dhaulagiri...one of the greatest of mountain gods
The grandeur of it...striking, regal, majestic...the wonder that I am here

Looking down, down after walking up for two days...mighty Kali Gandaki...earth's deepest gorge
Peering across at road trails...balanced on stone cliffs
Foot paths leading to higher and higher settlements...feeling safer looking up than down

A wedding band...giant horns at high places...announcing a procession to people in deep valleys
Drums, cymbals...reed sounding brass in minor key

Clouds, rippling the sky like stones on a pond...gathering, streaming out, feathering, rising
Clouds becoming statues...diamonds in the sun...hustled away by the winds
Cloud pieces in late afternoon rays...like stream ice at January thaw

Mountain Hawk shadows, diving, rising, moving silently away...surfing on invisible sky waves
Ocean sounds in windswept pines...tall and straight...tall and bent...sharply crackling
Leaning into each other like brothers and sisters
Fall seeds...scattered by the winds...carried by birds...dispersed by rivulets
Striving to insure life again
Fall seeds...from green leaves fading...fall seeds from yellow turning gold
From red to rust... from brown turning mahogany

Nepal is a strikingly beautiful country, all the more reason that the strife of the 1990's was so tragic. Unless one knows firsthand, how pushed to the wall the people of the region where it all began were, it is almost impossible to believe that such gentle, calm, and thoughtful inhabitants could end up in a bitter and devastating conflict with each other. Fortunately, these good people with such deep culture and long history finally overcame their differences. Development initiatives were put into place in an effort to correct regional deficiencies. Of course, there is a long way to go. This country which has long fascinated students of culture, eastern philosophy, and art from the west has become a busy destination once again for scholars and just plain tourists.

Valleys of huddled masses in the shadow of earth's most intimidating peaks
A people so poor yet so very giving – so much squalor next to such natural beauty
The pollution of industrializing places, outstripping infrastructure, in a land of fresh snow

New technologies amid the most ancient and complex of philosophical systems

Shocking hunger side by side with graceful saris and genteel customs
Gentleness and undying courtesy in crowds, traffic jams, and the frustrations of failing systems

Ancient palaces sprinkled through hovels of jobless peasants
Satellite dishes, cellular phones, email, and new high rises in a land of mountain runners
Flights from Singapore, Delhi, Frankfort, Osaka, Hong Kong, and Karachi landing in a place where people walk for days to get to their village
Intricate terracing and irrigation coupled with bullock plowing and hand threshing
Struggling Westminster institutions in a land of changing oligarchies
The mansions of new entrepreneurs rising in valleys with no roads, no power lines, no sanitation systems, and hand carried water

City streets crammed with bicycles, goats, human pulled freight trucks, and automobiles
Rickshaws, sacred cows, wandering dogs, and motorcycles
Great mysterious temples and involved ethics, long predating the new world
Pariahs among peoples of tolerance – nomads and wild tribes in a land of settled cultures

Smiles, singing, and sincere friends in a land of famine, natural disaster, and refugees
Mysterious soulful improvisation in a place of comforting fluted melodies
The destitute consuming discards in a land of ingenious cuisines
Holy riverbanks of squatters, swine, and sickness in a gentle place of great art and literature

Lives given over to preparation for eternity amongst broken bodies
Traditions of nonviolence overtaken by revolution and the overthrow of an ancient monarchy
Religion that binds to settled theology while liberating from the temporal and material

Great scholarship struggling up from masses of illiteracy
Finely chiseled faces and beautiful smiles next to grotesque images of mythical creatures

Open hearted welcomes and friendship for defiled barbarians in a place of closed communities
Incredible creativity within embracing convention

New sciences and accomplished astronomy coexisting with complex astrology and magic
Sacrifices, dirges, consecrations, penance, purification, and preparations for a holy state
Vishnu, Rama, Krishna and Siva – Brahmins and Chhetries with Sudras in the shadows
Gurus, priests, wandering holy men, mantras, and rites

Great mountainsides one can see clearly but could never get to.
And more – so very much more – how could it ever be?

TWO APPROACHES

There are two approaches to assistance for a country like this. Each is critical. One is down to earth socioeconomic development. The second is the development or revival of justice that reaches an entire population.

Socioeconomic Development

It is important that every routine need (i.e. for health, education, food security, infrastructure, transportation, government services, and opportunity to work) be examined to determine the extent to which they are, or are not, accessible to each population group with equity. Also, it is important that every routine need be examined to determine the extent to which it is, or is not, being made available to every population group with quality. Are some people able to have quality goods, services, and opportunities while others receive deficient seconds? Are available goods, services, and opportunities relevant to the critical needs of some, and irrelevant to others? From there one needs to identify causes of less than satisfactory situations, so that corrective interventions can begin to be designed. Reforms that stimulate development should eventually result in a country that has means enough, that its people can be treated fairly and have opportunities to build successful lives – if they have the will to identify and pursue opportunities. Those who take this approach would work in traditional fields of development but with the thought that a developed country can become systematically fair and just. They would address intervention, reformation, or upgrading in public and private sectors. Preparation for this work would entail becoming knowledgeable and skilled in a specialty of any of the applicable disciplines, e.g. health, education, agriculture, engineering, finance, and business.

Examples of Specific Projects to Which One Might Contribute as a Consultant

- Manage land use and agricultural improvement
- Reconstruct electricity generating capacity
- Re-develop public transportation
- Develop a regulatory environment
- Protect and manage natural resources

- Promote sound economic policies
-Promote business development
- Increase and control access to business capital
- Build effective education systems
- Develop healthcare systems
- Develop water and sanitation systems

Development or Revival of Justice

It is important that the lives of people of every ethnic and socioeconomic group, each gender, normal people, those with disabilities, those with education, and those educationally left behind, be examined carefully in relation to rights they have reasonable access to. Are the various groups within a country able to claim rights and resources through the system peacefully, without paying bribe money or some other tribute? Does the nation within which they live even provide a system for this? Are the governments where they live – national, provincial, district and community – respectful of and accountable to the people and do they advocate for them? Do the people live within a predictable system? Are the rules clear and do they apply to everyone equally? Do all people of every group in a country actually have protection of the law? On careful examination, is the law more likely to favor one group over another? Are any of the groups in a country especially vulnerable to violence, discrimination, exploitation, loss of employment, loss of property, or loss of citizenship? Indeed, does everyone born within a particular country have citizenship rights? Are there protections, within a subject country, of labor rights? Do any groups suffer labor abuse? Is everyone able, in some way, to have legal representation? Does the population have rights to clean drinking water? Is access to education for one's children the same for everyone? Is access to healthcare the same for everyone? Are there transparent regulations that govern commerce for everyone equally? Is justice systematic, transparent, carried out in the same way for all, and is it affordable? Evidence of the situation relative to these matters needs to be collected and analyzed so that corrective interventions may be designed. Preparation for this approach will require becoming knowledgeable and skilled in one of the specialties of law, justice, and security.

Examples of specific projects to which one might contribute, as a professional consultant

– The establishment of a constitution and other legal frameworks
– The development of police procedures
– The building of an effective and professional corrections system
– The establishment of independent courts
– The development of computerized administrative court records
– The generating of reforms for the legal profession
– The promotion of public understanding about the justice system
– The creation of political parties with professional procedures
– The development of voting procedures and reforms to ensure equal access to justice
– Assistance to civic institutions and NGO's to establish procedures and protocols, e.g. on offices, committees, duties, elections, meetings, and keeping records
– The reform of procedures and refinement of scopes of work for district government
– The refinement of free and responsible media

Needless to say, the two approaches above are not mutually exclusive. Each is critical. They complement each other and are interdependent. *Does this work interest you?*

Chapter X
The Promise of Technology

T here are developing countries where technologies that were common many years ago are not yet in place and other developing counties that, in some ways, are on the cutting edge. This is not to judge. For development to get ahead of where a people's interests and values are, to get ahead of the readiness curve, may not be sustainable. To get ahead of what a people can internalize, and make their own, may do more harm than good. To achieve what a host country will not be able to afford to maintain can be demoralizing. But it is probably better to err on the optimistic side than to be too conservative. Leadership on this, in some developing countries, is far ahead of what we in the so called developed world might have anticipated.

An Example of Convinced, Committed and Pursuing

Allow me to begin by sharing from an introduction to a proposed project.

"Another example of sophisticated forward-looking development in Jordan is the information technology sector. The government's policy is to give the information and communications technology market, incentives to contribute significantly to economic and social development by creating the legal, institutional, and commercial environment in which ICT is nurtured, grown, and sustained. Further, Jordan has committed itself to incorporating ICT into the daily lives of all its citizens. Efforts are underway to broaden access to ICT technologies to communities, business and families across the Kingdom. His Majesty, King Abdullah II, started this idea, establishing Jordan's Information Technology Community Centers.

And in partnership with the Ministries of Education, Higher Education, and Planning, the Ministry of Information and Communications Technology is proposing to establish a broadband learning and public access network to link all schools, colleges and universities. Such a network would be at the leading edge globally. In this connection it is important to note that secondary schools across Jordan already have fully equipped computer labs. Leading in this effort is the Ministry of Education, which has articulated a national e-learning strategy. The strategy is currently under implementation through the training of teachers, development of online curriculum and courseware and modernization of the learning process to enable innovation and creativity.

The role of teachers will be shifted away from lecturing to that of classroom facilitator whereby students will learn from a variety of sources in a variety of ways. Related to this, it is important to note that a group of high tech giants, including CISCO Systems, Hewlett-Packard, INTEL, Siemens, and Sun Microsystems are cooperating with the Ministry of Education to transform schools into model facilities where technology is at the service of learning and teaching and where information technology is perfectly integrated in education. The initiative will promote learning by discovery, innovative thinking, self-directed learning, experimental learning, life-long learning skills and habits, and self-reliance.

The Ministry of Information and Communications Technology and the Information Technology Association of Jordan has presented a report laying out a clear plan of action to bolster the country's nascent IT sector. It took a look at Jordan's strengths and weaknesses and outlined a five year plan to maximize the country's ability to compete in regional and global markets. The plan specified actions needed from government, the private sector and other stakeholders toward an Internet based E-economy. The nation will capitalize on its' young and well-educated population, who have excellent potential as tomorrow's global knowledge workers.[1]"

Impressive Leadership from Other Quarters

Many nations have learned how important keeping up with technology has become. Let me share two objectives from a plan still in draft. These reflect the intent of leadership that youth will stay abreast of changing economic and technological conditions.

That present and anticipated socioeconomic conditions in the country will guide the education system in preparing students to meet the challenges of the traditional economy, the future economy, and of society and the workplace

That attention to the implications of evolving knowledge, technology and innovation will guide the education system of the country in determining how to prepare students so that they may capitalize on opportunities in new or altered professions and businesses

Aspirations from Another Part of the Developing World

Many developing nations have made significant progress with the establishment of computerized management information systems. Allow me to illustrate plans to make such a system comprehensive and sophisticated by citing a section from a study labeled, *Organization and Policy Analysis, for the Directorate of Education, Government of the People's Republic of Bangladesh.*

"Regarding The Division of Education Management Information Systems – maintain data bases on all aspects of the system, e.g. school teachers and Teacher's College instructors, students, facilities throughout the system, equipment throughout the system, DPE personnel, field office personnel, auxiliary service institutions, e.g. NAPE, scholarship examinations and training. Manage, analyze and report data – and train managers to use it effectively. Manage a district based training program to promote data based decision making in line with the objectives on decentralization. Facilitate field level capacity in data management. Coordinate with the Bureau of Statistics and the Planning Commission. Maintain GIS data. Process research, planning, monitoring, baseline and program indicator data."[2]

Technology as a Tool in Development Projects

Not surprisingly, donor agencies are increasingly emphasizing technologies as a tool in their approach to projects. For example, USAID[3] has the following efforts underway in cooperation with host nations, in which technology plays a key part – Guatemala Rain Forest Alliance, Namibia HIV AIDS, Ecuador Coco Bean Project, Uganda Health Initiatives, Saudi Arabia Earthquake Zone Monitoring, Indonesia Environment, Clean Water and Hygiene, Tanzania Girls Science Camp, Kenya Household Gardening and Nutrition, Nepal Tiger Track and Protection Project, Albania Innovative Software Applications, Central Asia Project on Climate Change Related to Wheat Growth, Drought Tolerant Maize in Africa, The Use of Interactive Radio in Agriculture, Health Information Systems Upgrading, Information Systems Security, Research and Development on Microbicides and Vaccines, Technology

Based Solutions to stop Human Atrocities, Assistance to Improve Land Tenure Policies and Administrative Systems, Global Initiatives to End Hunger and Sustainable and Equitable Access to Land and Water.

Other Uses of Technology in Development

Many other things are being done in development that make judicious use of technology. For example, the World Bank[4] is promoting the internet and mobile phones for delivery of market information, financial services, and health services in remote areas. The Bank is also working in thirty countries in Sub-Saharan Africa to strengthen regulatory frameworks. The Asian Development Bank[5] is helping countries increase the use of ICT in key sectors. It estimates that 19% of its projects are developing and using ICT in transport efforts, 18% in public sector management, 17% in education, 11% in multi-sector projects, 9% in finance projects, 8% in agriculture projects, 6% in industry and trade projects, 5% in water projects, 4% in health and social protection projects, and 3% in energy projects. The Asian Development works in some 40 countries of Asia and the Pacific.

This is just a sample of the things being emphasized in technology for development. And these are just a small fraction of the organizations which are using and promoting the use of technologies in development. I have not mentioned the more esoteric technologies but if you have an interest and background in fields like body implants, genetic engineering, stem cell treatment, tissue engineering, laser video display, electronic sensing, wind turbines, solar power, wireless energy storage, machine translation, human/computer interaction, materials science, brain research, and so on, a donor organization somewhere may well have a need for people like you.

Small Scale, Decentralized and Environmentally Sound

The more common technologies used for development projects in teaching, agriculture, nursing, forestry, land use and conservation, environmental stewardship, energy generation, and so on remain very relevant. Technologies related to renewable resources, green building materials, transportation modes, sanitation and water treatment, housing, heating and cooling, and food storage are important in the developing world. In the interest of practicality, understanding, motivation, and sustainability, technologies emphasized by some in the field of development would be to the extent possible, small scale, decentralized, environmentally sound, and able to be managed and maintained by ordinary village occupants. There is need too for alternative energy technology (keeping in mind the range of energies available in the developing world), self-help technology, village level technology, cost efficient technology, and technology that is compatible with locally available materials.

Human Interaction, Communication, and Management Technologies

Often overlooked but very important to development efforts are the technologies that deal with human interactions, social structures, information gathering and decision making, motivation techniques, community choice, community participation, and influence and personal empowerment. Consider a discussion on this kind of human technology in the paragraphs below that are from a study on:

Leadership Consistent with Capacity for Professionalism and Responsibility

"It has been pointed out that many decisions seem to require approval at the highest level. This overloads senior officers and does not provide opportunities for others to get into substantive matters in accountable ways. It may be that initially, some poor decisions would be made further down in the system but without a chance to try or even to make mistakes, the performance of lower level officers cannot improve. As an example of a process that could be re-thought, note that horizontal consultation is discouraged by seemingly extreme vertical action. On several issues, matters are sent from bottom levels in the DPE through mid-levels to the office of the Director General. A file will be opened at the bottom of the official ladder, then pass through the Research Office, Assistant Director, Deputy Director, and Division Director. When the matter reaches the Director General, he or she may have a query or comment and the file is sent back down through the organization. Consultation takes place again at lower levels to develop a response and then communication is started upward again through to the Director General. Discussion amongst mid-level officers on professional matters could be considerably encouraged, if more decisions were made at lower levels. Centralized decision making can waste good talent and deflate and discourage professionals. If one's job consists of taking orders only, as someone said "do this and do that", then an organization is not going to get the value from them that it should. This is not just delegation but actually requires permanent shifts in authority. Certainly if the empowerment of Districts, Upazilas, and schools is to transpire, a considerable shift in management philosophy and practice will have to come into being."6

Authority Shared

The study of management tells us that authority shared will become more legitimate and accepted, making for a healthier, more positive, and productive organization. Theoretically, decentralized decision making contributes to people internalizing their work and becoming more effective and efficient. Control can be broadened in an organization so that employees become internally directed and are free (even eager) to act on professional judgment. A judicious sharing of responsibility, with authority, is important to the building of confidence such that people begin to take on (even look for) responsibilities without being directed to do so. It is important to note that some mid-level managers within the DPE would like this to obtain, "we would like to get our employees to the point where they will just do things." But the bureaucratic nature of the systems in place make it difficult for individual professionals to take on responsibility for much of anything from inception to its end. Even if supervision and management is enlightened and empowering, established layers of decision making can keep it from achieving as it should. It can be that a senior level supervisor has personal values which are consistent with modern management practices but cannot act on them. Supervisory behavior is in part, a reflection of one's values about the worth of colleagues. It is manifested in the degree of trust one displays toward others, receptiveness to and respect for other's ideas, one's openness, approachability, willingness to share decision making, and enthusiasm about initiatives by subordinates. As in any organization, there is considerable natural talent within the system in Bangladesh. However, it is constrained by the nature of decision making that seems to be firmly imbedded. Supervision in the system is tightly coupled. Most significant actions by officers are at the direction of a superior. This limits initiative and can contribute to alienation and even subversive behavior. Tone, management style, enthusiasm, commitment to profession, trust, expectations for employee performance, recognition, and psychological reward can bring an organization to life. But even if leadership is supportive of empowering management like this, the system within which it operates can make it impossible. There is need for education professionals within the system to be liberated. This is especially so in an organization where leaders at the top change so often. At present the organization is debilitated when there is change at the top. Everything has to begin anew. But if the majority of decisions could be made at the point of action, progress could continue."

Closing Thought

Perhaps you are interested in one of the technologies mentioned in this chapter. I would encourage you to study project designs which a donor or implementing organization may share with you, or which you may obtain from an archive. You will be able to pick out discussions of technologies that are part of various development efforts. Technology will increasingly become a key part of development initiatives.

1. *May Rihani and Donovan Russell, The Red Sea Project, Aqaba Special Economic Zone, Kingdom of Jordan, 2004*

2. *Donovan Russell and Anwarul Haque, Organization and Policy Analysis, People's Republic of Bangladesh, 2005*

3. *The USAID Website, Section on What We Do, Washington , DC 2013*

4. *Christine Zhen-Qiang, Information Communications and Technology, World Bank Website, July 2009.*

5. *Asian Development Bank, Website Section on Fighting Poverty in Asia, Inset Communications Technology, 2013.*

6. *Donovan Russell and Anwarul Haque, Organization and Policy Analysis, People's Republic of Bangladesh, 2005.*

Chapter XI
Development Management

Context

Your field of expertise may be any number of things: a special area within Healthcare, Education, Agriculture, Environmental Conservation, Justice and Development, Management Information Systems, ICT, Small Business Development, Integrated Rural Development, Human Rights, Democratization and Legal System Development, Disaster Relief, Refugee Assistance, and so on. In any specialty you may have a short or long term assignment, you may work as a counterpart advisor or have a stand-alone assignment, e.g. the installation of a laboratory machine. You may be engaged in start-up activities or you may be engaged in activities related to making an overall project effort sustainable. In some cases, people who have gained considerable experience, who have been well received by host country counterparts, who have been recognized as being especially creative and productive, and who are known as persistent and committed, are requested to take on an assignment in development management.

Development management consists of a broad range of work but for the sake of simplicity, let us lump it into three broad categories (1) Program and Project Design (2)

Implementation Administration (3) Monitoring, Evaluation, and Quality Assurance.

Program and Project Design

Country Paper – There are any number of things in which you might become involved if called on to be a team leader or team member for program or project design. You might, for example, join a team of host country professionals and others to do a country paper which is a broad study of all sectors in a nation and which examines all major challenges and opportunities for the country. Your team would likely look at problems, challenges, and opportunities related to things like natural resources, human resources, education levels compared to skill needs, health conditions and challenges, cultural factors, labor availability, soil, water, mineral and weather facts, trade, financial mechanisms, challenges and progress related to governance, migration, refugee populations, land tenure, population growth, law and order, disputes with neighboring countries, participation in international agreements, and efforts, development work that is on –going in the country, international covenants and obligations, national goals, progress toward goals, an examination of institutions that are working in national development, long range national plans, and international partners in the country's development effort. Your team would present a multi sectorial baseline view from which specific sector programs and projects would later emerge. The work can be fascinating.

Sector Assessment – Or you might be called on to lead or join a team that would do somewhat similar work but with greater depth in a single sector of the economy, culminating in identification of specific areas needing urgent attention. Your team would do in depth research on every aspect of one sector. You would study the situation, progress made in the sector, and causes of continued short comings. You would analyze and draw conclusions. Your analysis would be related to value perspectives of importance to the country, things like equal opportunity, access to services, the quality and relevance of institutional services to the needs of citizens, leadership, and governance, institutional management, and the policy environment. This effort would lay the ground work that planners lean on as plans for priority development programs or projects are developed. Let us look at the table of contents of a sector assessment.

Sector Assessment

Executive Summary
Purpose
Methodology
Major stages

System Overview
Students
Teachers
Curriculum
Schools and Facilities
Governance and Management Structure
Resources and Finances

Assessment
Successes
Access and Equity
Quality and Relevance
Enabling Learning Environment
Governance and Management

Conclusions
Priorities
Next steps

Discussion

A brief look at a completed assessment may lead one to see various challenges. For example, perhaps schooling is mostly teacher oriented. Perhaps the emphasis in the curriculum is not consistent with the goals the country has for a changing economy. Other findings could indicate, for instance, that school facilities vary significantly and given the fast growth, many schools are in rented facilities. There are disparities in facilities across the system. The management structure throughout, from Ministry to Regions to Schools, is fairly top down and is quite fragmented. The percentage of the GDP provided for public education is about average for the region in which the country is located. The nation has pushed hard to see that all young people have access to schooling and has been very successful in this. This has resulted in rapid growth in public sector schools. As often happens, coping with rapid growth can distract from efforts to maintain quality and indeed the quality of instruction is not as leaders in the sector wish. In addition to the quality of education being less than leaders wish, the curriculum emphasis does not make instruction as relevant as desirable, i.e. it is not well aligned with needs in the economy for higher technical and managerial skills. The learning environment in many schools does not seem to encourage adequate student participation. This has a number of implications for the skills and attitudes needed in a knowledge economy and for leadership in an increasingly global economy. The management and governance of education has not resulted in satisfactory community or parental participation or internalization of education as belonging to them. The Sector Assessment will have identified many areas of reform priority, organizing them into categories, e.g. leadership, teaching and learning, access and inclusion, learning environment and support systems, community relations and governance, management and policy. It may have noted the importance of seeing and dealing with them as an integrated whole. The study analyzes each area of challenge and identifies root causes of deficiency. It also looks at key functions of a good education system. Finally, the Assessment will suggest next steps to address the challenges identified.

Project Paper – As a Manager of Development working in the area of program or project design, you might also be called on to work as leader or team member in the development of a blueprint for a comprehensive project in a sector. Here you would build on the two efforts described above, i.e. (1) country paper research and (2) specific sector assessment and problem identification. Your team would select matters to be addressed. It would state objectives for the intended effort, identify necessary inputs and actions, and stipulate intended results. The project paper would become a critical and specific guide for those who ultimately manage a project that is envisioned. Your work on the blueprint would describe the sector and its setting, note players that would need to be recruited for the effort, specify areas of work responsibility, and lay out plans to be followed on matters like selection of outside managerial and technical help. The blueprint would be a guide for those who would ultimately write proposals to do the work and for those chosen to manage project implementation. It would speak to a range of pertinent issues, e.g. selection of implementing organizations, selection of personnel, costs, further plans needing to be developed as part of a project, training intended, organizational reforms, host country to donor relations, covenants, counterpart relations, and authority on various future matters. The blueprint is a plan of intended work. Let us have a look at the table of contents for a specific Project Paper.[1]

Project Paper

I Development Setting
a) The Country and its People
b) Education – Past and Present
c) Government Policies and Strategies
d) Employment

The section on employment presents the current situation, notes projections, and states goals from an analysis of the annual country plan and the sector assessment. It relates to the changing economy, country resources, population growth, new technologies, and employer managerial and technical talent needs. The information on employment is instructive to project planners in terms of the kinds of education and training that need to be made available.

II Project Rationale and Description
a) Problem Identification
b) Project Rationale
c) Project Description
d) Project Relationship to Country Development Strategy
e) Relationship of Project to Projects of Other Donors
f) Cost Implications
g) Analysis and Summary
 1. Economic Analysis and Summary
 2. Socio/Cultural Analysis and Summary

III Project Administration
a) Project Management and Coordination
b) Evaluation and Monitoring
c) Implementation Plan
d) Waivers
e) Contracting Considerations
f) Initial Environmental Examination

IV Annexes
a) Letter of Request for Assistance
b) Project Approval Message
c) Logical Framework
d) Technical Assistance Scopes of Work
e) Economic Analysis
f) Social Soundness Analysis
g) Cost Estimates and Budget Notes
h) Training Plan
i) Illustrative Commodity and Equipment List
j) Other Donor Assistance
k) Statutory Checklist

The project paper is critical to project proposals that will be written. Together with the project proposal that is selected, it becomes a blueprint for development personnel, counterparts, and both host and donor decision makers. It explains reforms to be made, training to be done, etc. It will guide work and decision making. Implementers will follow it closely in terms of preparing scopes of work, hiring, and planning actions to achieve goals and objectives. It becomes a guide for detailed planning on such matters as costs and budgeting, hiring and purchasing, construction, supplies and materials, areas of responsibility, covenants, approvals, change orders, counterpart relations, contributions, and specific work planning. It will also be a guide to evaluations.

Project Proposal – depending on the sector and the complexity of work needing to be done, design research and planning of several other types might be assigned. However, I will conclude this section on Program and Project Design by speaking to the project proposal, which is an indispensable part of project or program development. A request for proposals by the host country and cooperating donor is based on the country paper, sector assessment findings, and on the explicit project paper. Essentially, a request for proposals asks interested development organizations to propose and explain exactly how they would accomplish the goals and actions specified in the project paper. It asks that interested development organizations explain exactly what they will do and how. It also asks them to provide evidence of their capabilities and of any subcontract organizations that are being proposed. The request for proposals asks for a cost estimate on work to be performed that is detailed out. As a Manager of Development with experience in Program and Project Design, you could well be asked to prepare a project proposal. This is not something that one does alone. This also brings us to the intersection of the three major functions in development management, i.e. project design, implementation administration, and monitoring and evaluation. If done well, your proposal will win the project. The proposal will also become the work guide to the implementation team after the project has been awarded. Finally, it will play a role in monitoring, evaluation, and quality assurance because evaluators will look to it as a guide and series of benchmarks for measuring what has been accomplished.

Implementation Administration

Imagine that discussions between country leaders and their people have led to basic problem identification. This has led to collaboration between the country and development partners on in depth research and further problem explication. This work has culminated in the design of a project effort of high priority to the country. Based on this, the country, in collaboration with a donor partner, has requested that interested development groups submit a proposal on how they would lead and accomplish such a project. Imagine as well that one of the proposals has been chosen and you have been selected to lead it. What is your job? Based on the information in this section so far, you probably have a fairly good idea. However, allow me to make it more explicit by presenting some positions for you to reflect on. There are of course a great many types of development project, each being significantly different. The job of Chief of Party or Project Manager in each one will differ. There will though, be some common elements.

Example

Position: Chief of Party, Appointment of Four Years in Southern Africa

Responsibilities:

Support three districts on HIV/TB services by piloting new strategies and interventions in collaboration with national, regional and local health authorities. Work will include scaling up a project that will promote movement on clinical and organizational issues, e.g. further integration and decentralization.

Assist in selection of a local team that you will lead
Elaborate tasks and guide project work planning
Establish budget planning and control
Manage reporting at every level
See that all project goals and objectives are addressed
Oversee measurement of accomplishment
Cooperate and coordinate with other project officers across the country
Collaborate on community patient initiatives
Base initiatives on scientific evidence, promote lessons learned
Network with research institutions and participate in operational research programs
Develop a new project for the period immediately following your tenure
Participate civically with authorities and stakeholders on related efforts

Qualifications:

Physician with degree in public health
Clinical and public health experience
Expertise in HIV and TB in Africa
Substantial management experience
Experience with human resource and project cycle management
Intercultural sensitivity and communication skills
Capacity and interest in networking, knowledge sharing, and scientific exchange
Team leadership abilities
Fluent English, good writing skills; solid computer skills

Example

Position: Chief of Party, Appointment of Five Years in South America

Responsibilities:

Work closely with a Ministry of Agriculture and international collaborators to facilitate coordination of regional programs and communications between the Ministry, regional contractors, and donors related to projects which exist to improve operations and growth in the sector.

Manage program start up, monitoring, evaluation, and close out
Oversee all program management elements and provide senior leadership
See that project goals and objectives are addressed
Oversee measurement of accomplishment
Maintain regular and thorough communications with the donor and the company home office
Participate in selection of local personnel; train them on their project scopes of work

Manage all project planning responsibilities and oversee production of all work plans
Oversee all project advisors
Prepare project budgets and reports
Officially report to host government, the donor, and participating agencies and offices
Ensure compliance with home office and donor requirements, policies, and regulations
Interact regularly with host government counterparts on policy and strategic issues
Oversee team and counterpart work relationships
Represent the project to other donors, local governments, and community organizations

Qualifications:

Master's degree in agriculture science, agricultural economics, management, or related field
Ten years of responsible supervisory development experience to include:
> Direct supervision of professional and support staff
> Team building in a cross cultural setting
> Evaluation of staff performance and deliverables
> Contract management
> Five years in management of agriculture or business development and capacity building
> Supervision of monitoring and evaluation programs
> Experience in holding staff accountable for planned quality outputs
> Five years as Chief of Party or similar position
> Experience in multiple countries
> Excellent interpersonal skills
> Experience in communications with government, donors, and other stakeholders
> Three years of experience in design of agriculture programs

Experience with national policy reform and institutional capacity building

Professional presentation skills and concise writing skills

Ability to interact professionally and successfully with senior host country officials

Demonstrated organizational skills and considerable experience with deliverables

Capacity to resolve conflict

Experience on collaborative work with other projects and local partners

Demonstrated team building skills

Monitoring, Evaluation and Quality Assurance

To monitor is to watch, observe, and keep track of. To evaluate is to determine value, significance, or worth by careful appraisal. Quality assurance is to give attention to activities in the aggregate to insure adequate overall soundness and usefulness, i.e. good quality. A project or program manager has a need to monitor ongoing work activities in order to keep the endeavor for which he or she is responsible on the planned track. Such a manager will also be involved in internal evaluation and keenly interested in external project evaluation, because that will indicate the value and worth, in relation to planned outcomes, of what has been done through a project. Finally all parties, including those who will inherit and have responsibility to use a system productively, will be interested in the soundness for use of all elements of a system which has been developed.

A logical framework is commonly used by planners of a project. Planners use it to provide an overview of a project plan, showing alignment of the program goals in a sector with a project designed to help achieve them. The logical framework is also a step by step guide to implementers of a project, indicating appropriately sequenced actions to achieve intended outcomes. It is a useful guide for those who are charged with monitoring the progress of a project and to evaluators of achievement once a project has been completed. Logical frameworks can be developed for and used in any sector. They are organized in block fashion showing contingency relationships. The purpose in a logical framework is the effect which is expected to be achieved. The Goal is the highest level objective toward which a project is expected to contribute. The framework uses four columns. The first provides a brief narrative describing an event. The second lists verifiable indicators that the event has taken place. The third notes the intended means of verification. The fourth lists assumptions, i.e. external factors that could influence the intended events described in the narrative column. A logical framework presents sequenced activities and outputs. The logic used is that if (A) the activities listed are implemented and assumptions hold, then the outputs will be as listed. Further (B) that if the outputs listed are achieved, then the purpose will be achieved. And if the purpose is achieved, the high level goal will be achieved.[2]

[1] *USAID Team, BANFES Project Paper, Washington, USAID, 1984*
[2] *NORAD Group, Logical Framework Approach: Handbook for Objectives Oriented Planning, Oslo, MFA, 1999*

Chapter XII
Mission Organizations

What kind of development work do people with religious missions do and what are their motivations? Let us start with one of the most accomplished and celebrated of people, a gentleman who excelled in several fields. While there are hundreds of exemplars, I'll limit discussion in this section, to just a few of the outstanding people who gave of themselves to humanity in this special way.

Albert Schweitzer

"On the afternoon of Good Friday 1913, my wife and I left Gunsbach. At Lambarene, the Missionaries gave us a very hearty welcome. Unfortunately they had not been able to erect the little buildings of corrugated iron in which I was to begin my medical practice, for they had not secured the necessary laborers. The trade in Okoume wood, which was just beginning to flourish in the Ogowe district, offered any able African better paid work than he could find on the mission station. So at first I had to use an old chicken coop near our living quarters as my consulting room. By late autumn I was able to move to a corrugated iron building twenty six feet long and thirteen feet wide, with a roof of palm leaves, down by the river. It contained a small consulting room, an operating room of similar proportions, and a smaller dispensary. Around this building a number of large bamboo huts were gradually constructed for patients. From the very first days, even before I had found time to unpack my drugs and instruments, I was besieged by sick people. The choice of Lambarene as the site of the hospital was based on its location and on information of Mr. Morel the Missionary, a native of Alsace. It proved the right decision in every respect. From the distance of one to two hundred miles, upstream or downstream, the sick could be brought to me in canoes along the Ogowe and its tributaries. The chief diseases I had to deal with were malaria, leprosy, sleeping sickness, dysentery, frambesia, and phagedenic ulcers, but I was surprised by the number of cases of pneumonia and heart disease I discovered. There were also many with urinary tract diseases. Surgical treatment was called for chiefly in cases of hernia and elephantiasis tumors."

These were words of Albert Schweitzer on his first activities at a mission station in Africa. Dr. Schweitzer is of course well known but to refresh our memories, let me use the succinct introduction in the foreword to the book above, by President Jimmy Carter. The book is "Out of my Life and Thought."[1] President Carter wrote, "Albert Schweitzer brought to the early twentieth century, one of the most powerful and wide ranging intellects the world has seen. He not only studied but also mastered philosophy, music, theology, and medicine. He even became the world's authority on Bach and on organ building. Then Dr. Schweitzer demonstrated his gratitude for the gifts he had been given by devoting the majority of his life to relieving the suffering of the people of Central Africa. Despite an isolation that is hard to fathom in our age of easy communications, while in Africa, Dr. Schweitzer stayed current on the affairs of the world and provided commentary on ethics, war, nuclear weapons, and environmental degradation. His eclectic interests benefited not only Africa but the entire world." Although not mentioned in the foreword, Dr. Schweitzer won the Nobel Peace prize in 1952.

I suppose everyone who gets into international development does so on the basis of personal values that are very important to them. No doubt almost everyone in the field is committed beyond self and is dedicated to the service of others. Some are no doubt clearer on this than others. Dr. Schweitzer seems to have arrived at a decision to undertake such work after much thoughtful soul searching.

He was especially articulate about this. "Affirmation of life is the spiritual act by which man ceases to live thoughtlessly and begins to devote himself to his life with reverence in order to give it true value. To affirm life is to deepen, to make more inward, and to exalt the will to live. At the same time the man who has become a thinking being feels a compulsion to give to every will to live, the same reverence for life that he gives to his own. He experiences that other life as his own. He accepts as good, preserving life, promoting life, developing all life that is capable of development to its highest possible value. He considers all evil as destroying life, injuring life, repressing life that is capable of development. This is the absolute, fundamental principle of ethics, and it is a fundamental postulate of thought.

Until now the great weakness in all ethical systems has been that they deal only with relations man to man. In reality however, the question is what is our attitude toward the universe and all that it supports? A man is ethical only when life as such is sacred to him – the life of plants and animals as well as that of his fellow man – and when he devotes himself to helping all life that is in need of help.

Only the universal ethic of growing responsibility for all that lives can be founded solidly in thought. The ethic of relation man to man is nothing but a fragment of the universal ethic. The ethic of reverence for life therefore, comprehends within itself everything that can be described as love, devotion, and compassion in suffering, the sharing of joy in common endeavors."[2]

And on a slightly different theme, Professor Schweitzer expressed his motivation in the matter of sharing the knowledge of mankind, "If there is any ethical thinking at all among us, how can we *refuse* to let these new discoveries benefit those in distant lands who are subject to even greater physical distress that we are? Whoever among us has learned through personal experience what pain and anxiety really are must help to ensure that those out there who are in physical need obtain the same help that once came to him. He no longer belongs to himself alone; he has become the brother who will suffer"[3].

After a period away from Africa, Dr. Schweitzer returned in 1924. "All that remained of the hospital was the small building of corrugated iron and the hardwood skeleton of one of the bamboo huts. During the seven years of my absence, all of the buildings had decayed and collapsed. My life during the next months was lived as a doctor in the morning and as master builder in the afternoons. Then a severe famine broke out. The men who cut wood for timber all over the country had neglected the cultivation of the fields."[4] Again, Dr. Schweitzer is thoughtful and articulate about his mission work. "Because I have confidence in the power of truth and of the spirit, I believe in the future of mankind. Ethical acceptance of the world contains within itself an optimistic willing and hoping that can never be lost. It is therefore, never afraid to face the somber reality as it really is."[5] Finally, in the last years of his life, "I look forward to the future with calmness and humility so that I may be prepared for renunciation if it be required of me.

Whether we are active or suffering, we must find the courage of those who struggled to achieve the peace that passeth all understanding."[6]

Mother Teresa

Mother Teresa was born Anjeze Gonxhe Bojaxhiu in what is now the Republic of Macedonia in 1910. At the time, her birthplace was still part of the Ottoman Empire. After a long career she became founder of the Missionaries of Charity which consists of some 4500 sisters active in 133 countries. The organization runs hospices and special homes for people with HIV/AIDS, leprosy, tuberculosis, and other sicknesses. Services include as well, assistance to alcoholics and care for the blind. It manages soup kitchens, counseling centers for children and families, orphanages, and schools. It is also active in emergency relief campaigns around the globe. Members of the Missionaries of Charity adhere to vows of chastity, poverty, obedience, and to give wholeheartedly and freely to the poorest of the poor.[7] At the age of eight she lost her father and by the age of twelve she was determined that when age permitted, she would commit to the religious life, being especially fascinated by the work of missionaries in Bengal.[8] The girl destined to become Mother Teresa left home at age eighteen to join the Sisters of Loreto. She journeyed to Ireland where she studied, taught school, and learned English as it was the language of teaching for her order in India. She would never see her mother or sister again. She would eventually be fluent in Albanian, Serbo-Croatian, Bengali, Hindi, and English.[9] Mother Teresa arrived in India in 1929 and began her studies and preparations for eventual vows in Darjeeling, at the edge of the Himalayas. Here too she taught and studied for three years before taking her religious vows.[10] Later upon assuming duties at the Loreto Convent School in Calcutta she enjoyed teaching and eventually her duties as Headmistress of the school but became increasingly disturbed by events of the time, including the great Bengali famine and the outbreak of Hindu/Muslim violence. The city became plagued with despair and horror.[11]

In 1946, Mother Teresa answered a call of conscience and God to leave the convent and live among the poor of Calcutta. She adopted Indian citizenship, took further medical training and ventured into the slums. She initially started a school, took care of abandoned children and began tending to the needs of the destitute and starving. After a time, she was joined by a group of women and the foundation was laid for a new religious community to help the poorest of the poor. Income to support the work of the new community necessitated that she beg for food and supplies.[12]

In 1950, Mother Teresa received Vatican permission to create the Missionaries of Charity. Its work in her own words would be "to care for the hungry, care for the naked, the homeless, the crippled, the blind, the lepers, all those who are unwanted, unloved, uncared for; people who have become a burden to society and are shunned by everyone."[13] Over the years Mother Teresa received many honors and accolades, among them the Nobel Peace Prize in 1997.

Let us briefly look at some of what Mother Teresa said in the book, _In Her Own Words_, as an insight on her motivations, philosophy, wisdom, and commitment.

Make us Lord, worthy to serve our brothers and sisters who are scattered all over the world, who live and die alone. Give them today, using our hands, their daily bread. And using our love, give them peace and happiness.

Without a spirit of sacrifice, without a life of prayer, without an intimate attitude of penance, we would not be capable of carrying out our work.

Peace and war begin at home. If we truly want peace in the world, let us begin by loving one another in our own families. If we want to spread joy, we need for every family to have joy.

If we were humble, nothing would change us – neither praise nor discouragement. If someone were to criticize us, we would not feel discouraged. If someone were to praise us, we would also not feel proud.

At the moment of death we will not be judged according to the number of good deeds we have done or the diplomas we have received in our lifetime. We will be judged according to the love we have put into our work.

War is the killing of human beings. Who can even think that it could ever be just.

Peace begins with a smile.

In the developed countries there is a poverty of intimacy, a poverty of spirit, of loneliness, of lack of love. There is no greater sickness in the world today than that one.

To listen to someone who has no one to listen to him, is a beautiful thing.

David Pieter Faure

In the mountains of Transylvania a new religious movement emerged and the first edict of religious toleration in history was declared in 1568, during the reign of the only Unitarian monarch in history, King John

Sigismund. He was a frail and artistic person as well as being an accomplished linguist. The King was deeply interested in religion and worked to pacify area conflicts between Roman Catholics, Greek Orthodox, Lutherans, Calvinists, and Unitarians. Transylvania became the freest country in Europe in religious matters. The first decree of religious toleration was followed five years later when the young King issued the Act of Religious Toleration and Freedom of Conscience. In both the sixteenth and seventeenth centuries, Unitarianism appeared in scattered European locations. A Unitarian community in Rakow, Poland for example, flourished. Persecution followed the movement and the leader of the Polish group was burned at the stake. In 1791, scientist and Unitarian Minister Joseph Priestly of England had his laboratory burned and was driven from the country. Priestly fled to the United States and established churches in the Philadelphia area.

The first reference to Unitarianism in Africa was during British colonial rule in the Cape Colony of South Africa. Cape Town was visited by Raja Rammahan Roy, an Indian reformer in 1831. A prominent Cape Town Newspaper objected to his Unitarian views. In 1839, William Porter arrived in Cape Town to take up the position of Attorney General of the Cape Colony. He had been admitted to the Bar in 1831. His father was a leader of the New Light movement within the Presbyterian Church of Ireland. All of Porter's brothers had become Unitarian Ministers. Porter's progressive background could be seen during his tenure as Attorney General in the Cape Colony. In 1857 he drafted a color blind franchise for the Cape Colony constitution and he pushed hard for equality before the law of all colonists and the native population. One could say he was 130 years ahead of the time, as he opposed white injustice to blacks and deplored English speaking people's attitudes toward Dutch speakers in the Cape. Resigning as Attorney General in 1865, he became founder of the University of Cape Town, becoming Chancellor in 1876.

During this time, David Pieter Faure was preparing for a life and a profession that would go far toward needed reforms in the Colony. Faure was born in Stellenbosch in the beautiful Cape Colony in 1842. He was of proud Huguenot heritage and his family belonged to the Dutch Reformed Church. He studied at the University of Leiden in Holland where he experienced Professors with views that were quite different than those with which he had grown up. He studied matters of human justice and theology. During his life, Faure was a theologian, pastor, translator, social reformer, writer, and newspaper editor. He was the right person for the time when reform minded Unitarians became active in the British Cape Colony. In fact, he was the founder of the Unitarian Church in South Africa. One could say that as a clergyman in remote South Africa, he was also a missionary for theologically based reforms in society. Faure's Unitarian congregation was formed in 1867 after he returned from the University of Leiden in Holland. He ministered there until 1897 during which time he was active as a pastor, councilor, and reformer. This period of his life saw a great struggle on a host of watershed issues, e.g. language of official business, land struggles, government and settler strains, land rights, power sharing between the British Empire and her colonies, slavery, penal settlement, individual land rights, freedom of speech, relations with native peoples, social relations, and the influence of foreign education on South African Orthodoxy. It was a time of unrest for native populations, resistance by settler farmers of government regulations, hunger, and even starvation within certain ethnic groups. Consistent with his values and religious convictions, Reverend Faure was a major champion of the people on these and other issues. Attempts to marginalize various unfortunate groups during the period would have been more successful if Faure had not been their tenacious defender. He suffered serious ostracism and even death threats. To some Faure was a pariah, to others he was a hero of enlightened thinking and the courageous defender of dignity and human rights.

Faure was a clergyman on permanent mission within turbulent Southern Africa until his death in 1916.[15]

William Booth

William Booth was born in Nottingham, England in April of 1829. In 1842, when William was 13, his father sent him to work as an apprentice pawnbroker in the poorest part of Nottingham. In September of the same year, his father died. His mother had to take work in support of the family. Young William began to attend the Broad Street Methodist Church in 1844. Having been impressed by great preachers among the people of the streets, William began to deliver some of the sermons. He continued to support himself at the shop to which he had been apprenticed. William eventually became a Methodist minister. He and his wife Catherine founded the Christian Mission in London in 1865. A few years later, the name was changed to the Salvation Army. Eventually the Salvation Army was organized in the fashion of an army with ranks, disciplined functions, uniforms, its own colors (flag), special music, and most importantly selfless service to others. His religious campaigns became more than preaching, becoming accompanied by services for the poor, sick, disadvantaged, elderly, and counseling for the addicted.

The Salvation Army began to expand outside of the United Kingdom, first moving into Europe and the United States and into many of the countries of the British Empire, e.g. Canada, Australia, New Zealand, India, South Africa, Jamaica, etc. By the time of William Booth's death at age 83, it was established in 58 nations. It was to grow rapidly until it is now established in some 126 countries.

William Booth was also a prolific writer, regularly publishing a magazine and authoring several books. He was, additionally, a composer of songs. In 1890, a book of his became a best seller. A major theme of the book was that given the economic and social situation after the industrial revolution, it could be argued that England's working classes were no better off in quality of life than the people of many developing countries. The book, _Darkest England and the Way Out_ in part spoke to the need for social programs that were later established. The book proposes the application of Christian principles and the work ethic, together with critical social uplift programs. For example, the book suggests the need for training centers where the jobless and prospective immigrants would gain critical skills and work habits that would make them employable. It suggests places for the homeless to live, farm communities where the urban poor could be trained in agriculture, homes for fallen women and released prisoners, aid to the very poor, and help for addicts. It speaks to the need for legal assistance for the poor, together with the need for them to have banking provisions, access to health clinics, and industrial schools. Not surprisingly, Booth's activities and thoughts were controversial and raised substantial and sometimes violent opposition. In the end though, he and the organization created were highly respected. In fact, he became renowned among many world leaders.

The Salvation Army grew until today it is recognized as an essential part of society in many countries. It has roughly 16,000 outposts and churches spread across the world, bringing some form of assistance to nearly 3 million people. It has in the neighborhood of 17,500 officers, over 100,000 employees, and more than 1 million soldiers. There are hundreds of shelters for the homeless, a great many disaster rehabilitation centers, and many addiction dependency programs. It is well known for elderly services, prisoner rehabilitation, missing persons work, and youth camps. Most of what is done could be considered development, although there are current initiatives that are expressly labeled international development. Among these are initiatives related to inequalities and injustices faced by women, the development of water resources, work on behalf of a billion of the world's hungry through assistance to agriculture, interventions to shift the balance of the world's income by investing in activities and enterprises that reduce impoverishment, initiatives that address human trafficking at both source and destination points and community programs that give hope to the youngest generations. The Salvation Army is an indispensable partner at the site of every major world disaster. It is of course, recognized for its established goodwill and thrift stores, its soup kitchens and shelters, and its Santa charity work. Something perhaps not well known are the schools, training centers, clinics, the college, and the Ethic Center maintained by the Salvation Army. This Center does serious research and training and publishes widely. It engages in issues of the day related to Ethic considerations.

At the death of William Booth in 1912, 150,000 people filed past the casket. The following day 40,000 people, including Queen Mary, attended his funeral service.

Ignatius of Loyola

Born in 1491, Ignatius of Loyola was from a Basque noble family. His initial vocation was that of Spanish Knight and military leader. After being wounded in battle, he was inspired to leave military life and devote himself to spiritual pursuits with service to God and his fellow man. He was taken by the pure dedication of St. Francis of Assisi and other great monastics. Preparation led to hermit life followed by several years of formal study until he entered the priesthood, became a theologian, and founded the Society of Jesus. Between 1524 and 1537, Ignatius studied theology in Spain and France. He developed spiritual exercises, consisting of 200 pages of meditations, prayers, and mental exercise that would be performed over a 30 day period and which are used to this day. In Paris, he became leader of seven outstanding scholars who joined him in solemn vows to a lifetime of work, poverty, chastity, and obedience. In 1539, they formed the Society of Jesus, known across the world now as the Jesuits. Ignatius wrote the constitution of the society. The society became officially recognized as an organization that would do missionary work for the church. Ignatius was chosen as First Superior General of this religious order. The work of the Jesuits during his lifetime was widespread and highly respected. He died in 1556 of malaria. After a life of great achievement for the church and his fellow man, Ignatius was beautified and then canonized in 1622.

The Jesuits are known for scholarly and social justice work. They are highly educated and have become many, working across the world in challenging settings. Let us briefly examine one of them. Saint Francis Xavier was perhaps closest to Ignatius. They were roommates in seminary in Paris and Francis was the first to join the work envisioned by Ignatius. Francis was born at the family castle of Navarre which is now in northern Spain, in 1506. As was often the case with sons of nobility, he was destined for an ecclesiastical life. In 1525, he became a student at the University of Paris, the theological center of Europe. After all of the members of the group who had taken vows together had completed their studies, they reassembled in Venice. As a result of their teaching and work with the sick throughout Italy, they became highly sought after by the people and by princes of the time. Francis had an especially spectacular career of service. During his lifetime he taught, counseled, worked with the poor and sick, and established schools in many villages of Goa and other parts of eastern India followed by work with the Macuans of the southern coast of the country. Thousands of people followed him. In 1545, he travelled to the Malay Archipelago to work among the population at Malacca, and later among the Moluccas of the Spice Islands. In 1548, he returned to India where more

Jesuits joined him. In Goa, the College of the Holy Faith was taken under Jesuit management. Francis developed it into a center for the education of native Priests for the Diocese of Goa which stretched from the Cape of Good Hope in southern Africa to China. Francis also served for a period in Japan. He died at Sancian Island in China in 1522 and was canonized in 1622. Saint Francis Xavier is recognized as one of the greatest missionaries in history.

Throughout the years, the Society of Jesus has worked through many dedicated missionaries and there are presently some 24,400 members in 112 countries. They are organized into 1,825 houses. The Jesuits operate 90 colleges in 27 countries as well as 430 high schools in 55 countries. They teach virtually every subject and are known for high quality instruction. As a small indication of their contribution, five of the eight major world rivers were charted by the Jesuits, many of the world's astronomical observatories are Jesuit run, the Gregorian calendar was developed by Jesuits, and the long disputed Russo Chinese border was negotiated by Jesuits. In preparation for their life's work, Jesuits study theology, philosophy, languages, the sciences and math, and other subjects over a period of 10 years. In all, preparation before ordination is up to 15 years. In addition to preaching and counseling, Jesuits work as physicians, professors, lawyers, social workers, etc. Of course, the most recent occupation of a Jesuit is Pope. Not only is Argentinean Cardinal Jorge Mario Bergoglio the first Jesuit Pope, the new Pope Francis is also the first from the southern world.

Because education is such an important part of Jesuit work, it is no surprise that it has been particularly well thought through. The founder realized that critical and healthy changes in society could be encouraged through education. Many Jesuits since, have refined the Jesuit approach to education. Ignatius saw education as a means to help students freely chose to care about others. Jesuits believe education has the potential to free a person from biases, enabling free choice; it can help people become mature, i.e. people who care about others and about the world around them. Jesuit graduates should have made commitments to values, and should have acquired the self-discipline to live by them. They should tolerate diversity of perspective and have strong respect for their own cultural traditions. They should want good things for others as much as for themselves. This free and mature thinking has placed Jesuits in danger from despots on several occasions. Somehow, powerful people can be threatened by such thinking. Several Jesuits have been imprisoned by such people. Jesuits teach love and concern for each other, especially for the poor and those whom unjust structures of society keep oppressed and destitute. This is the obligation of educated and mature human beings.

Given that Jesuits often work in less than democratic settings, the subject of oppression is addressed in much of what they do. Oppression as social or as institutional or as systematic, i.e. whereby arrangements make it harder for some groups to excel than others, has been addressed many times in societies where Jesuits work. Some have been removed from their work in despotic settings and unfortunately, some have lost their lives to despots.

In this context, what was called liberation theology was a movement advanced by Jesuits in particularly oppressive countries, mostly in Latin America. The movement was controversial and not supported by everyone in the Jesuit hierarchy. Essentially those supporting liberation theology maintained that the church should get its legitimacy from promotion of the poor. The church should be a vehicle by which those who have been denied their rights, have been thrust into poverty and deprived of full status as human beings, get a hearing and hopefully redress. It was thought that the church should act to bring about social change and should ally itself with the working classes. In the seething world of Latin America half a century ago, this was an uncomfortable position. Individual Priests took on various social and political involvements and some moved from the houses of the order to poverty stricken areas, where they lived with the very poor. Those in the church who opposed Liberation Theology did not disagree that the poor and disadvantaged needed to be lifted up, that the oppressed needed voice. They did though, disagree with the church advancing these causes primarily through partisan politics or by action that could lend itself to social violence.

In parallel with Liberation Theology, various clerics and scholars of the time made great strides in other ways for the less advantaged. Ivan Illich, born in Vienna in 1926, studied theology and philosophy at the Gregorian University in Rome, served as pastor of a parish in New York and thence was assigned Vice Rector of the Catholic University of Puerto Rico where he organized a training center for American Priests on Latin American culture. Illich was also founder of the Center for Intercultural Documentation in Mexico and began research and teaching on institutional alternatives to technological society. He wrote the controversial book, *De-Schooling Society*, which took the academic world by storm, as well as *Celebration of Awareness, Tools for Conviviality and Medical Nemesis*. Dr. Illich's work was designed to contribute to mankind's unfolding. His writings have a liberating effect by showing entirely new possibilities, opening a door that leads out of routinized, sterile, and preconceived notions.

Also in parallel with the work of Liberation Theology, Paulo Freire made a significant contribution to thought on the oppressed. Born in 1921 in Recife, Brazil, Freire became intimately acquainted with poverty during the great depression. Freire enrolled at the University of Recife in 1943, studying law and philosophy. He taught in the public schools and in 1946 was appointed Director of the Department of Education and Culture in the state of

Pernambuco. In 1961, he was appointed Director of the Department of Cultural Extension at Recife University. In 1964, a military coup resulted in his being imprisoned. Later he worked at Harvard University and at the Food and Agricultural Organization of the United Nations. He also took an assignment as advisor on education to the World Council of Churches. He believed there is no such thing as a neutral education process and that education functions to either facilitate integration and conformity of the generations, into the logic of the existing system, or it becomes and advances the practice of freedom, and the way in which people deal critically with reality, discovering how to participate in the transformation of their world. Freire promoted an education that would allow the oppressed to regain their humanity, and in turn be able to overturn their condition. They would need to play a prominent role in their own liberation. His writing is very relevant to those who would work in the international development field, and in my opinion, is critical if we are to do more good than harm.

Churches with International Mission Organizations Include the Following:

United Methodist Church Disaster Relief and Response
475 Riverside Drive
New York, New York 10115

Baptists on Mission
205 Convention Drive
Cary, North Carolina 27512

Presbyterian Mission Agency
100 Witherspoon Street
Louisville, Kentucky 40202

Catholic Relief Services
228 West Lexington Street
Baltimore, Maryland 21206

Church World Service, Development and Humanitarian
Assistance
Box 45 110 Maryland Ave N.E Suite 108
Washington, DC 2002

The Episcopal Church in America
Global Justice 815 Second Ave.
New York, 10017

Unitarian Universalist Service Committee
689 Massachusetts Avenue
Cambridge, Massachusetts 02139

American Friends Service Committee
1501 Cherry Street
Philadelphia, Pennsylvania 19102

Church of the Nazarene, Global Ministry Center
17001 Prairie Star Parkway
Lenexa, Kansas 66220

The United Church of Christ
Global Ministries
700 Prospect Avenue
Cleveland, Ohio 44115

Seventh Day Adventist
Office of Adventist Mission
12501 Old Columbia Pike
Silver Spring, Maryland 20904

Evangelical Lutheran Church in America
Global Mission
8165 West Higgins Road
Chicago, Illinois 60631

The Lutheran Church, Missouri Synod
Missions and Outreach
1333 S. Kirkwood Road
St Louis, Missouri 63122

Lutheran World Relief
700 Light Street
Baltimore, Maryland 21230

Church of the Brethren in Christ
302 Lake Street
Huntington, Indiana 46750

Mennonite Central Committee
211 South 12th Street P.O. Box 500
Akron, Pennsylvania, 17501

Church of Latter Day Saints
55 East, North Temple Street
Salt Lake City, Utah 84150

Assemblies of God, World Missions
1445 North Boonville Avenue
Springfield, Missouri 65802

United Pentecostal Church International
Global Missions
8855 Dunn Road
Hazelwood, Missouri 63042

African Methodist Episcopal Church
Service and Development Agency
1134 11th Street N.W.
Washington, DC 20001

The institutions above are within sects of the Christian tradition. If you have an opportunity to look through publications or websites of these or others of a similar nature, you will find each has its own unique development and relief program. Together, they do a great amount of disaster relief and refugee assistance. They also have an impressive array of development programs. For example, you will find an emphasis on meeting basic needs for families, caring for displaced people and helping them get a new start, long term actions to ameliorate hunger, work to transform communities, youth empowerment, education, and training. You will find descriptions of work on the underlying causes of poverty so that people may become self-sufficient. Some programs take a holistic and integrated approach, leading to an expansion of economic opportunity, interventions related to getting at least some education for children, safeguarding the health of mothers and their children, advocating for effective social and political policies, ending gender based violence, helping communities adapt to climate change, enhancing access to water, and improving water management. At least one major institution works widely on problems with respect to addiction, child adoption, aging, corrections, psychological counseling, disabilities, homelessness, parenting, and housing. Another has many programs including one with an emphasis on immigration issues. Some of them engage in work on what they call the root causes of poverty and on agriculture, preparing for the results of climate change, promotion of civic participation, and the insurance of continuing livelihoods. There are those with medical teams and disease research. Major efforts have been on HIV/AIDS, Malaria, and infectious diseases. In the literature one can read about initiatives labeled human dignity and rights, landmines, chemical and nuclear weapons, active peace, justice, and corporate responsibility. Others focus on support for the millennium development goals, the environment, energy, and food security. Some list their guiding principles and you will find they include but are not limited to, discussions on the sacredness and dignity of human life, the common good, the social nature of humanity and its effect on human potential, individual rights and responsibilities, the inherent dignity of all creation and stewardship, the solidarity of the entire human family, inherent value, the most vulnerable, and decision making as close to the people as possible. Several of the denominations work on before and after conflict peace-building. In the literature, one finds descriptions of education for peace, conflict prevention, conflict resolution, peace with justice commissions, women and peace-building, reconstruction, the relation of micro-enterprise development to peace, peace research, demobilization, post conflict communications, trauma healing, citizen diplomacy, and intervention roles. Other development programs include gender justice, indigenous and minority rights, responsibilities for natural resources, fair trade, youth outreach, awareness on the underlying causes of poverty, and full citizenship.

Needless to say, there are many development initiatives within other religions. Relief activities are common and thoughtful development work is ongoing. Listed here are some resources in case readers would like to explore this further:

The Baha'i Faith
Baha'i National Center
1233 Central Street
Evanston, Illinois 61201

Buddhist Relief and Development
Linda Learman, Buddhist Missionaries in the Era of Globalization
The University of Hawaii Press, Honolulu, 2005.

Hindu Relief and Development
Samvadk@gmail.com

Jewish Relief and Development
Jews for Peace, Social Justice, Equality and Human Rights
Suite 550 Oakland, Ca. 94612 info@jewishvoiceforpeace.org

Islamic Relief and Development
PO Box 22250 Alexandria, Va. *22304 tel. 855-447-1001*

1. *Albert Schweitzer, Out of my Life and Times, Baltimore, The Johns Hopkins University Press, 1998 p.136.*

2. *Ibid, p.157*

3. *Ibid, p 195*

4. *Ibid, p.207*

5. *Ibid p. 243*

6. *Ibid p. 244*

7. *Encyclopedia Britannica, Blessed Mother Teresa, 2007*

8. *Vatican News Service, Mother Teresa of Calcutta, Rome, 200*

9. *Joan Graff Clues, Mother Teresa of Calcutta, Chelsea House Publications, NY 1988 p.24*

10. *Ibid p.31*

11. *Kathryn Spink, Mother Teresa, Harper Collins, NY, 1997 p.18 -22*

12. *Joan Graff Clues, Mother Teresa, Harper Collins, NY, 1997, p. 35*

13. *Paul Williams, Mother Teresa, Alpha Books, Indianapolis, 2002 p. 62*

14. *Mother Teresa, In My Own Words, Liguori Publications, Missouri 1997*

15. *George E. Carter, The Life of David Pieter Faure, A Unitarian in South Africa, The Edwin Mellen Press, Lewiston, NY, 2010*

16. *Encyclopedia Britannic, Saint Francis Xavier, London, 2013*

17. *Yamiche Alcindor, Jesuits: An Order of Education and Social Justice, USA Today, Washington, 2013*

18. *BBC Religions, Liberation Theology, The BBC, London, 2013*

19. *Ivan Illich, Celebration of Awareness, Penguin Books, New York, 1971*

20. *Paulo Freire, Education for Critical Consciousness, The Seabury Press, New York, 1973*

Chapter XIII
Natural Resources and Security
Development and the Web of Existence

I Suppose the natural environment of a people combined with their beliefs and convictions, generates behaviors which affect the stewardship, conservation, and the technical applications they practice, and this helps to determine individual and even national security.

Might this be a career in international development that you would like to investigate? What does it involve? Could it be related to your interest in agriculture, climate science, wildlife management, forestry, environmental conservation, natural resources, energy, parks and tourism, water resources, mining, desertification, or oceanography?

Terms of Relevance to the Discussion in this Chapter

<u>Nature</u> – a creative and controlling force in the universe.
<u>Stewardship</u> – the individual responsibility to manage one's life and property with proper regard to the rights of others and one's progeny.
<u>Conservation</u> – planned management of a natural resource to prevent exploitation, destruction, and neglect.
<u>Conviction</u> – a strong persuasion or belief.
<u>Sustain</u> – to give support or relief, to supply with sustenance.

<u>Stake</u> – an interest or share of an undertaking.

<u>Balance</u> – an aesthetically pleasing integration of elements, an equipoise between contrasting, opposing, or interacting elements.

<u>Develop</u> – to promote growth, cause to unfold, to expand, to become gradually manifest. <u>Neglect</u> – implies giving insufficient attention to something that has claim to one's attention, to give little attention or respect.

<u>Destroy</u> – to ruin the structure, organic existence, or condition of, to annihilate or vanquish.

A WEB OF EXISTENCE THAT REQUIRES BALANCE

Consider a Scenario

Human energy, creativity, and perhaps even optimism and constructiveness are affected by the physical and mental health of individuals. This in turn is at least partly dependent on nutrition, sanitation, and hygiene. Sanitation and hygiene are affected by belief, education, and infrastructure. Nutrition is dependent on the food people have to eat and the water they have to drink. Food and water can be affected by understandings within countries and by agreements between nations. They are also dependent on climate, land tenure, systems of commerce, and farming. Farming is beholden to land tenure, available finance, training and education, access to technology, a reliable supply of irrigation water, the availability of un-eroded soil, dependable seeds, and predictable climatic conditions. Farming is also dependent on there being consumers of agricultural products who have the wherewithal to purchase. This implies some sort of system that makes it possible for such people to exist. When people live where some of this web has broken, where something critical is unavailable, unpredictable or insufficient, any number of unfortunate things can transpire. There might be the loss of a healthy, secure, and productive human population. There might be conflict over necessary resources. As we have seen many times, conflict can eventually lead to the displacement of thousands, even millions. It is not surprising that displaced people living in despair as unorganized transients or in someone else's country as refugees are easy victims of exploitation. One result can be social instability which might go on for generations, as children of school age miss the opportunity of an education and families have little hope. Instability may engulf not just the unfortunate but sooner or later, everyone of a region. The trust and confidence that enables a people to live side by side in peace and justice can, under such circumstances, disappear for long periods.

Consider a Second Scenario

Living, for most people, demands work. Having productive work necessitates that people have knowledge and skills useful in their setting. These are gained from one's family or in schools and colleges. Having a job that makes a reasonable living possible is also dependent on there being places to work. Predictable and productive places of work are possible when things like legal, financial, health, energy, transportation and natural resource matters, and infrastructures are organized, regulated, and in place. Good jobs are most likely to be established where healthy, constructive, aspiring, cooperative, and talented workers are plentiful. Being able and willing to live in a place, especially with a family, is more likely if good food, hygiene, sanitation, and cultural amenities are affordably available. Having reliable sanitation, hygiene, and food is dependent on having a healthy and productive environment in terms of temperature, soil, and water. An environment that is self-regenerating is dependent on stewardship rather than exploitation – stewardship that is enlightened about matters like the effect on water conservation and air quality from healthy forests. Having reliable sources of food for a population is also dependent on productive agriculture that does not destroy its environment. Having convenient goods and services can depend on there being reliable transportation as well as affordable energy. Energy for living is indispensable but if not carefully planned and used, can be destructive. It is a fascinating web of existence that requires balance.

One could go on with these scenarios. However, the intent is to focus attention on how very dependent and interdependent we are in terms of climate, soils, water, forests, energy, crops, and other people.

And so given this web, conceptually isolated development efforts in relation to forests, crop farming, pollination, farm animals, energy, climate, water use, conservation, irrigation, erosion, and air quality, are overly restrictive. Development efforts have become more integrated.

Many people are interested in a career which embraces this kind of development. Let us briefly review some efforts that are relevant:

NEW AND BROADER CONSIDERATIONS ON SECURITY

1. ***A Voice of America Video in News/Africa*** on 05/20/2013, and internet printable, reported on a global water systems project that coordinates and supports research to study complex water systems with interactions between natural and human activity. This is an analysis of the extent to which humans have affected the environment, the damage done, and what can be done to correct it. Titles of related articles reported by VOA are: *Toxic Waste Exposure Widespread in Developing World, Fish Thermometer Reveals Impact of Climate Change, Forests and Trees Key to Food Sustainability, Earth and Moon Share Water Source.*

www.voanews.com/global-water

2.*The USAID Climate Change and Development Strategy*, January 19, 2011, Print Brochure, Bureau for Policy, Planning and Learning ,Washington, DC, explains that a major goal on climate and development, is to enable countries to accelerate transition to climate resilient, low emission development that promotes sustainable growth. www.usaid.gov/our_work/policy_planning

Excerpt – (a) *Increasing resilience to climate change* – "some 2.5 billion people depend on climate-sensitive economic activities such as agriculture, fisheries, forestry, and tourism for their livelihoods. Climate change impacts in the form of rising temperatures, increasingly variable rainfall, stronger storms, and sea level rise are likely to undermine these livelihoods and threaten food security and public health, especially in developing countries where USAID works. USAID, by helping countries withstand and bounce back from climate change impacts, plays a vital role in preserving economic opportunities and ensuring access to food and health services in spite of a changing climate.

Excerpt – (b) *Promoting low emission economic development* – "According to the International Energy Agency, in 2008 greenhouses gas emissions from developing countries exceeded those from developed countries for the first time. Over the next thirty years, more than 90 percent of projected growth in global energy demand will come from developing countries. Investing in low emission development that leapfrogs traditional carbon-intensive energy sources and supports clean, efficient solutions benefits both the environment and global economic growth and helps create new markets for US technologies."

3. A paper, by the Thomson Reuters Foundation, printed 05/30/3013, labeled *Climate Adaptation Policy*

Crucial to Easing Conflict, suggests that "Most conflicts in modern times are intrastate, often fueled or financed by natural resources. The University of Uppsala's Armed Conflict 1946 -2011 database, shows 26 of 27 armed conflicts globally were intrastate while the UN Environmental Program's *From Conflict to Peace Building report, approximates that 40 percent of civil wars have been associated with natural resources.*"

www.trust.org/item20130530095414

4. ***A research paper published by the British Overseas Development Institute*** in 2013 suggests that natural disasters and climate, induce vulnerability, which is exacerbated by inter-clan conflict.

www.odi.org.uk.

5. ***Research by the Center for Climate and Security*** suggests that a significant factor in Arab Spring uprisings was climate, in that climate change caused severe drought and shortages of water, thus greatly increasing food prices, 2013.

www. American progress .org.

6. We of course have viewed water over the centuries in terms of being necessary to human consumption and crop irrigation. People in development are seeing it now in new ways. Let me quote from a Thomson Reuters Foundation paper of February 22, 2013: ***Shared Rivers and Aquifers Face Strains from More Demand.*** "One hundred forty five countries share river basins with neighbors and need to promote cooperation over a resource likely to be disrupted by more frequent floods and heat-waves. In the past few decades, definitions of security have moved beyond a limited focus on military risks and conflicts. About 185,000 Somalis fled to neighboring

nations in 2011, driven largely by water and food shortages linked to drought. While in the Sudan, whole communities were forced to leave due to water scarcity. Water supplies are under increasing stress from a world population of more than seven billion which is likely to reach nine billion by 2050. The damaging impacts of climate are most often seen in water. Floods in Pakistan in 2010 killed almost 2,000 people and droughts in the US and Russia in recent years have driven up global food prices. Water related diseases, from diarrhea to malaria, kill 3.5 million people every year, mostly in developing nations. Watersheds, lines that separate neighboring drainage basins, cross the territories of 145 nations. There are over 300 trans-boundary aquifers from which groundwater can be extracted. Each person needs between 50 and 100 liters (13 to 26 gallons) per day to meet basic needs."

www.trust.org/itemwater

7. *A USAID paper, Advancing Water Supply, Sanitation and Hygiene,* notes that 800,000 children under five die from diarrhea each year and 88 percent of diarrhea is attributed to unsafe water. The paper goes on to explain how USAID water programs address the problem. "USAID water programs support enabling policies and frameworks, develop institutions, expand access to financially sustainable services, and promote behavioral change. Projects build the capacity of both small scale service providers and larger utilities, improve household and community hygiene and sanitation, partner with a range of public and private organizations, and engage with national governments for lasting change."

www.usaid.gov/waterandsanitation. 05/2013.

8. *The Global Footprint Network* works to advance the science of sustainability. It is engaged throughout the world. Its initiatives are many. Let us briefly examine one,

Footprint for Nations. The organization notes that in today's world where humanity is already exceeding planetary limits, ecological assets are becoming more critical. Each country has its own ecological risk profile. Many are running deficits, with footprints larger than their own biological capacity. Others depend heavily on resources from elsewhere, which are under increasing pressure. In some parts of the world, the implications of ecological deficits can be devastating, leading to resource loss, ecosystems collapse, debt, poverty, famine, and war. The ecological footprint is a resource accounting tool that helps countries understand their ecological balance sheet and gives them the data necessary to manage resources and secure their future. The organization suggests it is almost certain that countries and regions with surplus ecological reserves – not those relying on continued ecological deficit spending – will emerge as the sustainable economies and societies the future.

www.footprintnetwork.org/en/index.php/GFN

9. A paper called **USAID's Strategy** notes that on climate they have three main priorities of assistance (1) helping countries adapt to climate issues (2) helping them mitigate, i.e. helping to curb growth of carbon emissions, invest in clean and efficient energy, and support sustainable land use and (3) integrate climate change knowledge and practice into all USAID programs to ensure that all sector portfolios – agriculture, energy, disaster preparedness, democracy and governance, health, and others are climate resilient and when possible curb greenhouse gas emissions.

www.usaid.gov/globalclimatechange. 05/2013.

10. **The Asian Development Bank** funds and manages development projects in every sector. It is understandable that they are concerned about energy in Asia as well as the

pressures of such a heavily populated region on the environment.

www.AsianDevelopmentBank.org.

A SAMPLE OF ASIAN DEVELOPMENT BANK PUBLICATIONS

New Energy Architecture in Myanmar 06/2013 (an analysis to help understand the nation's current energy challenges)

Addressing Beijing Air Pollution 05/2013 (recommends short and long term policy measures)

Assessment of Greater Mekong Energy Sector Development Progress 04/2013 (an update on regional energy resources)

Improving Agricultural Productivity and Rural Livelihoods 04/2013 (documents experiences in agricultural development in Asia)

Asia's Energy Challenge 04/2013 (relates the energy challenge to exceptional growth in Asia)

Clean Energy Investments 03/2013 (summarizes Asian Development Bank investments)

Economics of Reducing Greenhouse Gas Emissions in South Asia 03/2013 (what can governments do to influence clean energy in member nations?)

Clean Energy Financing Partnerships 02/2013 (summarizes progress)

Planning of Solar Park to Mitigate Risks for Investors 02/2013 (summary of a success in India)
www.adb.org/publications/search/338

ANOTHER TYPE OF SECURITY

11. <u>Another type of security</u> is having enough to eat. Nearly one billion people in the world go to bed hungry every night. By 2050, the world population is projected to reach 9 billion. It's said that to adequately feed that number will require a doubling in agricultural production. That would mean increasing production by that much in just 37 years. Also, given the extent to which the world's land and other resources are presently used, it would seem that to accomplish the goal, we will have to somehow become much more efficient. What exactly is food insecurity? It means among other things, not having a diet necessary to adequate nutrition. It means the insecurity that accompanies hunger or fear of hunger. It means not having a diet necessary to family health and it may mean prolonged undernourishment that stunts growth and cognitive development. Surely this too can be a source of community, nation, or even regional instability. Food production of course is uneven across the world. Even so, overall the increase of basic foods has kept pace with population growth in recent decades. This may have changed of late. It requires study. International development organizations and agencies have focused on agricultural production and have made significant strides in recent years. However, the challenge remains. It is heartening to know that government and foundation donors, together with NGO's and nations themselves, recognize the challenge and are cooperating on ways to more efficiently and adequately produce food. Of course, irrespective of the quantity the world achieves, there is always the problem of some having more than enough good food and others being on the edge of starvation. That goes

beyond the production challenge. *A paper labeled "Agriculture and Food Security distributed by USAID", last updated on April 10, 2013, notes the basic approach they are taking to fight hunger and increase food security around the world.*

www.usaid.gov/what*wedo/agricultureandfoodsecurity*:

– Invest in scientific and technological agricultural research
– Develop agricultural markets to help farmers sell products at a profit
– Help farmer's access capital
– Offer extension services so that farmers know the best techniques
– Develop strategies to help countries feed people without depleting natural resources
– Provide emergency food assistance

12. *The farmer to farmer program* is an initiative whereby volunteer farmers, extension personnel, cooperative leaders, farming organizations, and agribusiness personnel spend time helping farmers in developing countries on very practical matters.

www.usaid.gov/ourwork/agriculture/farmertofarmer

13. *Our demands on the world's resources are unsustainable.* Ecosystems, including rivers, lakes, coral reefs, forests, grasslands, and marshes provide essential resources that provide food, water, shelter, and energy. These ecosystems are significantly threatened. The problem is made worse by climate change, driven by the use of fossil fuels and deforestation. Development agencies are helping hard pressed countries to cope. For example see: www.usaid.gov/whatwedo/environment. This was last updated in 02/2013.

14. Switching emphasis just a bit, let us consider efforts to develop biofuels and use them in clean and efficient ways. *Cornell University* is engaged in many initiatives across the developing world. Scientists from the Department of Crop and Soil Sciences of the College of Agriculture and Life Sciences, together with colleagues from several other faculties at the University, are engaged in research that will provide answers to many fundamental questions about biofuels, their potential uses, best practices related to their production, and their environmental impact.

Let us note just a representative few of the questions being addressed by the Cornell research. Can corn energy yields be increased while reducing fertilizer costs and maintaining soil and water quality? Can corn production be increased without increasing emission of nitrous oxide, a potent greenhouse gas? What are the environmental benefits and greenhouse gas reductions from using dedicated grass bioenergy crops as solid versus liquid biofuels? Can grass pellets be burned efficiently in pellet stoves while meeting air quality standards? How will various bioenergy crops affect soil nutrient cycling? How will they affect soil carbon sequestration? Various types of biomass can be used to produce energy using low temperature pyrolysis. This produces bio char, a form of charcoal. How much can bio char reduce emissions of greenhouse gases, such as nitrous oxide and methane, from soils? With respect to oil crops for biofuels, what are the optimal management techniques for high yielding varieties? The conversion of cropland to produce biofuels may pose a serious threat to food security in many countries. How can countries with limited food reserves, increase both food and biofuel production? How will different bioenergy systems affect soil, air, and water quality?

css.cals.cornell.edu/cals/css/research

15. A critical part of the discussion about our use of natural resources to meet needs, while at the same time minimizing

environmental impact and being fair to stakeholders, must be the world's forests. A very significant and comprehensive study on this is called *Sustaining Forests, A World Bank Strategy*. The most expedient way to indicate what it is about is to quote the introduction by Maurice Strong, then Chairman of Earth Council. "In many parts of the world, the remaining great natural forests – and the many Biodiversity treasures they harbor, are at risk, from agricultural and grazing expansion, excessive exploitation, uncontrolled wildfires, and a number of other well- known causes. People who depend on these forests for important elements of their livelihood – and these include many of the poorest and most marginalized communities in the world – are facing a grim future, if these forests continue to degrade and disappear. Sustainable national economic development, the viability of natural land and water systems, and the stability of the global climate itself, are also directly connected to forest outcomes. The World Bank, along with other members of the international community, is engaging comprehensively with partners from civil society, governments, the private sector and the donor, and scientific communities to deal with this problem. We must acknowledge that protection and sustainable production must go hand-in-hand in forests, and that all legitimate interest groups must have a voice and a role in the use and protection of these forests, and in rebuilding and rehabilitating them. This booklet constitutes a major step in rethinking our strategy and developing an integrated and innovative approach to deal with the complex political and institutional issues involved, as well as the technical and investment priorities."

www.worldbank.org/forests

RESOURCES

The major bilateral donors fund many types of development projects, including projects on the topics of this chapter. If you are interested in a career on this you would find it instructive to explore literature or websites on each of these. They are:

Government Donor	Approximate No. of Countries in Which Active
United States Agency for International Development	120
Japan International Cooperation Agency	72
U.K Department of International Development	27
Dutch Ministry of Foreign Affairs	33
Norwegian Ministry of Foreign Affairs	114
Spanish Ministry of Foreign Affairs and Cooperation	50
Agence Francaise de Development	65
Canadian International Development Agency	all of the developing countries
Swedish International Development Cooperation Agency	44
Australian Agency for International Development	Asia, the Pacific, Africa, Latin America; Middle East
Danish Ministry of Foreign Affairs	15

Gesellschaft fur Internationale Zusammenarbeit	130
Belgian Ministry of Foreign Affairs/Development	19
Swiss Agency for Development and Cooperation	Asia, Africa, Latin America and the Middle East
Finnish Ministry of Foreign Affairs	14
Kreditanstalt fur Wiederaufbau	75
Irish Department of Foreign Affairs	15
Italian Ministry of Foreign Affairs/Development	100
Korea International Cooperation Agency	110
Luxembourg Ministry of Foreign Affairs	10
New Zealand AID Program	18
Austrian Development Agency	16
Greek Ministry of Foreign Affairs	10
Portuguese Institute for Development Support	7

In addition there are a great many implementing organizations, i.e. NGO's, service organizations, universities, corporations, charitable organizations, and international agencies. Should you wish to explore some of them, let me suggest that you start with those which are members of an organization called Interaction, located at 1400 16th Street, Suite 210, Washington, DC 20036.

Its website is www.interaction.org

Interaction

Interaction has a membership of some 180 large and not so large NGO's that work across the world. They work to eliminate extreme poverty, uphold human rights, safeguard the planet, and to ensure the dignity of the poor and vulnerable. Their goals include to make the world a more peaceful, just, and prosperous place. The range of programs fall under humanitarian action, advocacy, international development, and NGO accountability. Some of them work in the implementation of large scale contracted national development projects. Some of them focus on a select group of countries and build a relationship with them over many years. Funding for their work is from many sources. Members focus on various agendas. For example, these include economic and social development, relief to victims of disaster and war, assistance to refugees and the displaced, human rights, democracy, gender equity, health, education, economic opportunity, climate change, the environment, agriculture, food security, population concerns, and more equitable, just, and effective public policies.

There are of course many other organizations you may wish to explore. Just two of them are:

The Society for International Development

This is an organization of some 178 members including Foundations, National Government Agencies, International Agencies, Consulting Firms, NGO's, Universities, International Businesses, Coalitions, Associations, Training

Organizations, Religious Relief and Rehabilitation Organizations, etc. SID works to advance equitable development by bringing diverse constituencies together to debate critical ideas, policies and practices that will shape the global future.

www.SID.org.

The Center for Global Development

This is an independent non-profit think tank that does rigorous research, actively engages the development community, pairs research with action and advocates practical policy innovations. The areas of focus include AID Effectiveness, Debt Relief, Finance, Global Health Policy, Inequality, Population and Development, Regions, Transparency, Capital Flows, Financial Crises, Economic Growth, Globalization, International Financial Institutions, Poverty, Technology, Climate Change, Education, Fragile States, Governance, Democracy, Migration and Development, Private Investment, and Trade.

www.CGD.org

Is this career for you?

Chapter XIV
Character, Beliefs, Convictions, and Practices
A Career for Me

I sincerely hope this book has answered questions that you had. Perhaps it has raised others that you are eager to answer for yourself. I hope you are more intrigued than ever by the possibilities of a career in international development.

What We Accomplish Will Be Determined By Character and How We Do It

Let me conclude by addressing the thought that in our work, the end is inherent in the means that we employ, that how we do something is as important as what we try to do. In the long run, whatever we accomplish will be determined by how we do it. Who we are in terms of sincerity, concern, integrity, compassion, and respect for the humanity of others will have a significant effect on the outcome of what we undertake. In large measure, the people with whom we work will be to us what we are to them, as ultimately we strive for mutual respect, appreciation, learning, trust, empathy, and in a fundamental way, oneness. How we work and relate of course, is dependent on our values, on what we stand for.

You know, whether we have an assignment as Project Chief of Party in the field, as an advisor who is working with counterparts, as a home office manager, or as a support specialist in an office thousands of miles away, we have contracted obligations for things like achievement of objectives, project checklists, timelines, regulatory compliance, etc. Those and other management duties are vital and can be very interesting and challenging. Because of the nature of development, we usually work to a western sort of business model. If we were not conscientious and responsible, we would not have the development position that we do. And so, it is understandable that we must give considerable attention to significant management responsibilities.

Sometimes though, we may become quite absorbed by the enforcer part of our responsibility. After all, a donor or donors may be spending millions on something we have a responsibility to see accomplished. Further, the people of the host country need to be benefitted. We do not want to waste resources that are so needed by them.

Also, given our scope of work and letter of appointment, we may find that we spend a lot of time vertically on business with the home office or with far away technical professionals whose specialty is what we are working on in this particular project. Moreover, the pressures of an interesting but complex project can lead us to spend a lot of our effort on the sort of tallying up role.

Balancing Management and Leadership

All of this is important but needs to be practiced side by side with the exemplar role, where we are able to model creative ideas, enthusiasm, positive workmanship, caring relationships, and dynamic leadership.

In development, we are assigned to work with nations, with well-established institutions, with struggling institutions, communities, villages, and local organizations. We need freedom and time in these settings to work side by side with our hosts in such a way as to demonstrate leadership integrity that manifests itself in things like inspiration, trust, fairness, responsibility, and commitment to the welfare of our staff. Having enough time for this is not easy.

Further, given our role, it is normal that we are looked to by our home office to sort things out in cases of possible corruption (which in the host culture may not be seen as corruption at all), in cases of conflicting interpretations or duties, in cases of favoritism, etc. This is understandable and in such matters and all responsibilities, we must consistently be seen as fair, objective and truly caring – *as wanting the best of results for all parties*. If that is our character, things will work out. In fact, problems we have to deal with may be seen as opportunities to demonstrate what we should be accomplishing with the project in any case. If we can achieve balance between routine management duties and leadership, the inspiration, innovation, trust, fairness, diligence, responsibility, and sense of service that we represent will come through.

What we represent may well make opportunities for our local colleagues to stand up to old traditions, which perhaps made sense in their original context - traditions which are outmoded but may be encouraging a few leaders, who see themselves as privileged, to continue old practices, e.g. the utilization of arrogance and coercion, the exploitation of workers, and the use of institutional resources for personal rather than community benefit. In the course of our work with partnering local colleagues, it can be useful for those who were born into a station or into a situation in which they feel compelled to accept practices they know are corrosive or unfair, to see that business can be conducted differently. If we spend all of our time on project work details, important as that is, we'll not have the opportunity to use who we are as a person, and the consideration and professionalism we normally employ in our work relationships, to maximum potential. *Whatever we ultimately accomplish will be determined by how we do it.*

On Gaining Understanding

It sometimes happens that well-meaning and highly educated development managers, or advisors, arrive at a project having thoroughly prepared themselves on what is to be done. Further, they have a strong professional background in the relevant field and have a clear picture of how project personnel should proceed. It is good to be well prepared. The thing of it is they are not the sole deciders. Ultimately, host country people will determine if a project truly gets off the ground, and will make success or failure possible. Given this, how can you get off to a promising start? One of the most important things one can do is to understand the lives of your hosts – what fills their plates, what do they worry about, what do they celebrate? Another matter of importance is to understand their customs – what constitutes civility, how should one behave, what are their traditions? Yet another consideration is to observe for the good things about them – admirable things about the national character, the hardships they as a people have and continue to overcome? Of what are they most proud? Another important thing related to gaining understanding and getting on equal ground is to gradually learn of their agendas, i.e. the formal agenda and the informal agenda of what they hope to get from your work together. In addition to the expressed project, are there other things they hope to achieve? Try to learn of their concerns related to your work together. Attempt to figure out what is truly valued in this new setting. Learn of the unique things about the history. Try to understand the fundamental ways in which your culture and theirs differ. Share their aspirations for the project and yours.

Beliefs, Convictions, and Practices

Remembering that what you accomplish will be determined by how you proceed (i.e. how you manage, how you work, how you relate) it can be useful to carefully think through (even research if necessary), and decide on those things you believe in related to how. For instance, what do you believe related to approaches beyond the technical? What do you believe related to types of leadership in cross cultural development settings? Are there decisions and courses of action that might weaken rather than strengthen the people who are supposed to be helped by a project? How do you know the present level of understanding or expertise of people who are supposed to receive help of a kind? What are your thoughts about concepts like host readiness and necessary preparations before proceeding with a project goal? What is your understanding of and beliefs about internalization? Are there ways a leader could actually inhibit or discourage internalization? If you already have a good understanding of the culture in which you will work, do you think local management will fit neatly with project procedures and practices? How will you fit them together? A significant part of almost any development project has, in some way, to do with learning. Do you have thoughts about levels, kinds, and practices in learning that might be more appropriate than others related to internalizing, incorporating, owning, or sustaining? Do you have views about management types which are most appropriate, in relation to helping clients sort out, decide on, internalize, and own? You will want to inspire and raise hope. Can you oversell – and if so what might be the long term effect on morale? If expatriate project personnel are affiliated with a home based institution like a University and are routinely tuned in to them, there may be a steady stream of new ideas, innovations, and such. Those are usually generated from work and research in a very different kind of environment. How might they be screened for relevance, practicality and acceptance in the administrative setting and culture of the project? What can be accomplished through relatively short term project engagement? What probably cannot be? What can be accomplished through long term project engagement? What might make a long term project more effective? We are blessed with many new devices and ways to communicate. Indeed we have been socialized to them. Some of us would not know how to work without them. What are your thoughts, even convictions about their use culture to culture? In what ways might technology bring us closer together in our tasks and relationships, in what ways might it keep us from being as close as we need to be? In the setting of the project on which you will be working, is this an either/or matter? In your opinion, what does it mean to truly get to know each other across cultures? What does it mean to work across cultures?

Some Fundamentals

The following are points for you to reflect on. They are beliefs that I hold about development.

a) For a reform to succeed and be sustained, host country people must be willing, able, and organized to make the improvements themselves. Some development assistance does not emphasize this. It attempts to lay on from the top. This removes the opportunity for a people to display initiative and to feel responsible – and may contribute to an unseen long term psychological dependency.

b) For the most part, professionals in development believe in long term host participation. This necessitates appropriate pacing. However, some professionals are overwhelmed by the momentum of their own organization or of their government. Excessive momentum can also be generated by professional themes that are in vogue in the donor country. Momentum may be the result of policy or sector research as well. Or it may result from developments in techniques and technologies or innovations in management. This is not to say that momentum is a bad thing but if one believes in genuine participation, it has to be managed.

c) Host country people cannot work meaningfully toward a development unless they have time to cope with its complexity, understand the organization it will require, and perceive an outcome that is compatible with their values.

d) Agendas imposed from outside can promote vertical allegiances that divert attention from the horizontal person to person, institution to institution or community to community collaboration that is critical to local decision making, ownership, self-reliance and to sustainability.

e) Laid on, bought, and paid for development, as opposed to deep rooted, shoulder to shoulder development, can mislead donors about accomplishment leading them to severely short circuit the time that true development takes.

f) The cafeteria style of development can lead to a periodic taking up of new themes, each one raising expectations, only to drop hosts further when the effort is replaced by something else. This is contrary to the systematic laying of foundations and the accomplishment of conditions necessary to being able to take the next appropriate steps, in reasonable measure and at the appropriate time.

g) People can only work productively in accordance with their readiness and preparation. As in anything, it is necessary to be fully accomplished at a level before being able to go further. Also, if an initiative employs techniques or resources that are not going to be available when donor assistance finishes, hosts will not be able to make it their own and sustain it. Working outside the long term capability of one's hosts can create unreal expectations and set them up for failure.

h) Bringing about meaningful, appropriate, and sustained change requires credibility. Credibility in development requires true partnerships where the problems and dilemmas of a people are understood and taken on through close and longstanding association, as if they were problems and dilemmas of the assistance personnel.

I) It is critical in development that host country people gain belief in themselves and faith in the predictability and possibility of accomplishment. This cannot be achieved from an expert's reports or through the gifts of a donor.

HE DIDN'T STAND IN HIS OWN WAY

Let's do this final section as a discussion. It will be the sort of discussion on a career in development you may have already had, perhaps more than once. Some readers may have had a discussion on heart felt matters like this, while employed in something else. Others of you may have had such a discussion while deciding whether or not to enroll in a graduate program in one of the specialties of international development. Others may have had talks on this general topic with colleagues or professors – or perhaps with field practitioners after enrolling in graduate school. The discussion that follows is a composite of such discussions I had long ago at the beginning of my career in development.

"I'm truly glad you could come up here Don. I've long hoped you might get to see this part of the Maritimes and our University." They were at Saint Francis Xavier University in coastal Nova Scotia. Don had just told his friend about the decision to do a Ph.D. at Cornell. However, Saint Francis Xavier had always intrigued him. He had known dedicated African leaders who studied there and who had returned home to take on special work in development. He thought of this small university as quietly at the forefront of some key development initiatives.

"So you will be leaving your position over there in late August, eh? It's been a pretty exciting run hasn't it. Not many people get a chance to do something like that." His friend was referring to the planning and reorganization in which Don had worked in the neighboring province. "Do you think you might want to direct provincial or perhaps national planning again one day?"

"Yes, if everything goes well, I hope to get back into this sort of thing, but if possible in a cross-cultural setting." His friend Ben knew Don pretty well and was not at all surprised.

There are some wonderful places in this world and Nova Scotia in summer is one of them. It has amazing rolling fields at the start of harvest, against the blue sea. They were near St. George's Bay which borders the Northumberland Strait and spectacular Cape Breton. Within an easy drive of enchanting seaside places, Chedabucto Bay, Arichat Harbour, Little Dover, Drumhead, Cape Canso, Broad Cove, and a host of others.

The University was founded in 1853. It was just up the coast from the first historic Pugwash Conference on Science and World Affairs. He first met Ben at a conference in Toronto. They were paired for various discussion groups and soon found lots in common. They could somehow really talk. What was it, the same spirit of adventure, similar values, an interest in the world beyond their doorstep?

Don was twenty nine. His friend was quite a bit older and had worked in Latin America and Africa. Don looked up to him for his service in difficult places and complicated situations. It seemed to him that Ben lived at a level of meaning beyond most people. Provincialism or materialism didn't shackle him. His life wasn't about career prestige. He didn't seem to have an interest in displaying how much he had accumulated, in any sense. His ego didn't own him. He didn't stand in his own way. From their talks, Don knew him to sincerely believe in the nobility of mankind. He firmly believed in the potential of the human race.

Being around Ben made Don search his own soul. Why would he go off to graduate school when there was so much to do, right now, in the world? Indeed his present work offered tremendous opportunities to contribute. What was this thing about getting a Ph.D. anyway, an ego trip perhaps? *Some people deal with their ego in one way – some another*, he thought. It bothered him. After all he had been one of those to question our way of living, our relationship to the earth's resources, and the unnecessary chase of credentials. He talked to himself about the degree and at times was convinced that it would simply help him better pursue his service goals. He worried that if he was ever going to do it, he needed to get at it. After all, he was already twenty nine.

Ben made a pot of tea. "Have you seen this?" he asked. It was a newspaper article on the major development projects in Canada. "With major experience in one of them and the knowledge you are going to get in the Ph.D. program, you'll be able to pursue things in a much larger arena. You'll likely be able to break into the international scene if you want. I know what you are thinking, Don. You think there is something incongruous about pursuing your own ambition and service to others. You're still young. That's a reasonable concern. In fact I'd worry about you if you didn't think that way. Purity of motivation is key. You are going to have to work at that – at doing whatever you do in life for the right motives.

As they had their tea, Don asked questions about Ben's work overseas. He was fascinated. There was the political intrigue that one gets caught up in, in a third world setting. They had discussed that before. Today they got way beyond that.

Ben spoke of the people in the third world he had worked with. "Look, I can't tell you how much I've come to appreciate them, to respect them. It always concerns me when a new initiative gets underway. So often, people from industrialized countries just don't know how to work in the third world. It's a sensitive thing you know, you can do more harm than good if you're not careful. I've seen it happen. You know how it is Don; you can even see it here or in the States. But, man, it's so much more pronounced across cultures."

A flock of seagulls landed in the end of the field they were facing. Why had they left the sea and the beaches? What if anything did it portend?

The two men sat quietly for a few seconds and then Don ventured a tentative opinion. "It sounds pretty daunting to work productively across cultures."

"Not at all," Ben replied. "It just takes understanding, tolerance for frustration, a deep appreciation for other cultures, and some technical know-how of course." He laughed at his own response as if to say, *that's a tall order, isn't it?*

"I'll tell you what; there is nothing more interesting, more intriguing, more fulfilling when you get it right. There is nothing more rewarding than a friendship across cultures. And believe me, it's totally fascinating to come face to face with an infinitely broad range of human possibilities – to realize, although perhaps not understand – that there are so many different ways of thinking and being in this world. To realize that our way of seeing things and handling life is in a tiny corner, is only a small part of this old world's possibilities. That's not to denigrate what we've inherited. I'm proud of it. But one can also marvel at and come to be proud of more of the human heritage. Let me tell you, it's marvelous to have to figure out what is behind behaviors that we've never dreamed of before, to have to learn how to manage and get things done in an entirely different setting, a different universe of beliefs and values and habits. To come to understand enough – that one sees there are many worthy and good ways that a society can be. I tell you, it can be mind-boggling. The opportunity to truly work in – not just visit or study – another culture is a great privilege."

Don was captivated by the topic. However, it was one of those situations where you don't know enough about the subject to ask good questions. At least that's how he felt. "I think you're pretty unique, Ben. I think it's more common for people to turn away, to avoid the so called third world – whether it's a third world within the borders of North America or someplace across the oceans. Why is that, anyway?"

Ben hesitated, reflected. "Oh, I don't know, I guess most people just get caught up in their thing. Just staying afloat in Canada is pretty consuming I guess. I suppose it's the same or more so in Western Europe. For sure, it's so in the U.S." He paused. "But then, there are those who would reject it out of hand. Beyond that, I guess there are people who are plain against it. Maybe it's best that they are not involved. I can't think that they would go about things in a very sincere or sensitive way."

Don found himself adding a comment. "Yes, we've all known individuals who refuse to get to know, or even see, people who might need a hand."

"More than that," Ben said, "we've all known people who actively avoid involvement with others by building myths about them – things like you can't trust that bunch anyway or they're the type who would take advantage of you. Perhaps some of the most stand-offish with respect to this sort of thing are in a way, threatened by it. They develop disdain, perhaps even animosity toward others because deep down it's uncomfortable for them to get close to misfortune or poverty or sickness."

Don added a small thought, almost shyly, "I think there's another reason that people don't get involved. It's too messy, too ambiguous – it doesn't meet their need for predictable boundaries. It's not black and white enough, there isn't the promise of neat closure."

Ben was noticeably pleased by the insight but said he wasn't sure most people see that far ahead. "Most probably don't realize how intriguing this work can get be, but that's why it is so fascinating." He agreed that rigid individuals might find cross-cultural work rather unappetizing.

Ben lit his pipe again. It seemed to go out frequently. Don wondered if he didn't keep enough tobacco in it or if he just forgot to puff on it. They decided to walk around the neighborhood. A woman was sowing grass seed in a newly spaded spot. It made Don notice how nicely landscaped most places were. Someone had done a lot of digging, a lot of planting, a lot of trimming. As they turned a corner, they came within the view of two dogs. Both were behind a fence. The little black one spoke its mind, barking and scratching the earth with its hind feet. The large brown one didn't pay them much attention. Its attitude was that of a yawn. It surveyed them lazily and then closed its eyes. An antique ford stood along the curb. Mint condition. "On second thought, I guess I don't feel comfortable about our conclusions Ben."

"How so?"

"Well, I suspect some perfectly secure folks reject involvement on well thought out ideological grounds."

"Hmm, I wonder," Ben replied. "I wonder how many. I'd rather think that most centered and focused people who don't get involved, are just too busy with other aspects of life." They caught each other's eye and realizing this had become too serious, they broke into laughter.

They wandered into a small bookshop. The woman behind a desk told them it was a temporary affair. "For the summer months only, all proceeds to charity. Here take a card. The charities are listed on the back." But then she began describing books in much more detail than they wanted. They would have liked to half-heartedly browse. Unfortunately, her intensity more or less drove them back to the street.

"Why do you care, Ben? What causes you to want to make a difference?"

"Oh man, what a question. First of all, let's make it clear. I'm not special. Millions of people in North America care. My life just happens to be organized in such a way that I can act on my caring. *But I care Don, because I can. Therefore I have a responsibility to.* Does that make any sense?"

"Not much I'm afraid."

"Well, look at it this way. Most of the world is still overwhelmed by daily toil just to survive. I know. I've been there. I've seen it. If you were born into an average family some place in Africa or in say Afghanistan or the valley of the Amazon, your days and years from childhood on would be so filled with back-breaking toil that you would have no chance to develop your innovative or creative powers. Haul water, hand mill the lumber, turn the sod, thresh the grain, spin the threads. Everything by hand. A job that a machine in Canada does in ten minutes might take you three months.

You know Don, but you don't. Everyone knows at an intellectual level how it is in the Third World. But unless they have been there, unless they have lived it, they really don't know at all. Even the lower classes here have been liberated from that. And we can read and write and use laptops. We have access to incredible information if we want. We can create. Except for the very privileged of the past, we are a first. And we have a responsibility to use this newfound privilege, this liberation, in a constructive helpful way. If we hoard it, it will disappear. Don't ask me how I know that. I just do."

As they approached a shady and grassy spot along the harbor, Ben changed the topic. He asked some pretty straight questions about Cornell. It was almost too intrusive. But they were friends. It was OK. Where would they live, how could it be afforded, what about the kid's schooling, did Don worry about the study pressure, how did he justify leaving such a good job? The answers were brief. Don was more interested in the conversation they had been having.

He steered the conversation back to Ben. Thinking back to early in the afternoon when Ben expressed concern about the harm that can be done through development work, he asked him how it could be avoided. After all, didn't people in the third world have something we've lost? How could we be of assistance without encouraging them to adopt the worst parts of our culture? "Well, let's put it this way," Ben said. "Sometimes we care so much that some of us would force people into seeing things our way." He gave a little laugh. "That's precisely the wrong way to go about helping someone. Also, we should not expect the poor to dream our dream. Sometimes that dream is totally out of the question for them and sometimes it is just plain inappropriate. At the same time, I think we have to be honest. Look, if you want this, you will have to do a, b, and c. You will have to become like that. You will lose x, y and z. And we have to see their ideas and values as worthy – as worthy as anyone else's. It's counterproductive to think we have it and they don't. That leads to the worst kind of prescriptive charity. Perhaps what we do with others someplace, will result in something far different than what exists in Canada or Europe or the U.S. That's fine. And perhaps we, the so-called helpers, will gain far more than those we work with. Perhaps we will be significantly improved as human beings. That's fine too. *Ultimately our work should help us see the good in each other. It should never be about indoctrination. It should never build things that will someday alienate people from their histories or from each other.*

But make no mistake about it. Development of one sort or another has always gone on. It's going on in Canada as we speak. It will always be happening. Extremely powerful economic and social forces have been unleashed in this world. Poor, unsuspecting, innocent, good people and societies can be bowled over by them. *We can help ameliorate."* Don was taken back a bit by this thought, *"we can help ameliorate,"* he repeated. "For instance," Ben said, "you know how here in North America we start projects with some form of need assessment or with something similar like research or perhaps a SWOT or something. That may be OK here but think about it in a very disadvantaged setting and in a culture very different from ours. Think about arriving on the scene and essentially asking your hosts to tell you everything wrong and everything they need. They have good intentions of course, but what does it essentially do? It says to them that they are backward and inferior and that they need you to find the path forward for them and a donor to pay their way. Not a good way to start. Better to learn from them about all they have going, the good things, the skills, organization within their community, the accomplishments, the admirable qualities, and the aspirations. Better to help them rediscover the good about themselves and the advantages they have. Then they can relate what they have and can do - to what they would like to achieve. This helps them begin to psychologically build on the positives, and to keep their dignity. Granted, there will be an inevitable gap between what they have or can get and what they need. There will be time enough to address that after they have realized all that they have to work with, all that they are as a people. To begin the other way around is to tell them early on that they are needy and your being there means there are resources and services available for them, if they can accede to how poor and unfortunate you or your organization thinks they must be. *What is wrong, what is lacking, will come out soon enough, but dynamics and self-image can be changed, if we start with what is right about them and with what they may be able to somehow engineer.*"

Ben's next words were drowned out by a car horn. Don was engrossed. He strained to hear, but Ben stopped and looked up. It was a friend they were to have dinner with. "Come on you fellas, jump in. Man does not live by ideas alone."

CPSIA information can be obtained at www.ICGtesting.com
Printed in the USA
BVOW05s1000120215

387404BV00001B/9/P

9 781621 373636